FOR:

FROM:

The unfolding of your words gives light.

Psalm 119:130

Daily Inspiration from the New International Version
Copyright © 2000 by The Zondervan Corporation

ISBN 0-310-98257-X

Requests for information should be addressed to:

🏛 ZondervanPublishingHouse
Grand Rapids, Michigan 49530
http://www.zondervan.com

Associate Editor: Molly Detweiler
Compiler: Pat Matuszak
Cover Photo: Shouichi Itoga/Photonica
Cover design: David Carlson
Interior design: Laura Blost

Printed in the United States

00 01 02 /OP/ 4 3 2 1

CONTENTS

INTRODUCTION

Learning to hear God's voice seems to come so easily for some people, while others struggle to hear a single word. There was a time when Samuel struggled to recognize the Lord's voice too. The first times God spoke to him Samuel thought it was Eli calling him (1 Samuel 3:4–8). Many of us hear the voice of the Lord but don't recognize it as his.

Learning to recognize the Lord's voice comes with practice. If we slow down and take time to listen, while also listening as others share godly wisdom with us (as Samuel heeded Eli's advice), we will grow in our ability to hear and to recognize God's voice. The important thing to remember is that God wants to communicate with us. From Genesis to Revelation we see him talking with his people. He wants us all to tune in. It's a vital part of the way we grow in our relationship with him and move into our destiny.

From The Christian Growth Study Bible

Daily Inspiration from the New International Version brings you an entire year of selected Bible readings on a variety of topics, helping you listen to God every day. Start at the beginning of the year on Week 1 or start in the middle of the year with a topic that interests you most. Any way you use it, *Daily Inspiration* will give you peace and encouragement all year long!

❧

MONDAY

"Come, all you who are thirsty,
    come to the waters;
and you who have no money,
    come, buy and eat!
Come, buy wine and milk
    without money and without cost.
Why spend money on what is not bread,
    and your labor on what does not satisfy?
Listen, listen to me, and eat what is good,
    and your soul will delight in the richest of fare.
Give ear and come to me;
    hear me, that your soul may live.
I will make an everlasting covenant with you,
    my faithful love promised to David.
See, I have made him a witness to the peoples,
    a leader and commander of the peoples,"
declares the LORD.

Isaiah 55:1–4

TUESDAY

Jesus, tired as he was from the journey, sat down by the well. It was about the sixth hour. When a Samaritan woman came to draw water, Jesus said to her, "Will you give me a drink?" (His disciples had gone into the town to buy food.)

The Samaritan woman said to him, "You are a Jew and I am a Samaritan woman. How can you ask me for a drink?" (For Jews do not associate with Samaritans.)

Jesus answered her, "If you knew the gift of God and who it is that asks you for a drink, you would have asked him and he would have given you living water."

John 4:6–10

WEDNESDAY

"Sir," the [Samaritan] woman said, "you have nothing to draw with and the well is deep. Where can you get this living water? Are you greater than our father Jacob, who gave us the well and drank from it himself, as did also his sons and his flocks and herds?"

Jesus answered, "Everyone who drinks this water will be thirsty again, but whoever drinks the water I give him will never thirst. Indeed, the water I give him will become in him a spring of water welling up to eternal life."

John 4:11–14

THURSDAY

"For my thoughts are not your thoughts,
  neither are your ways my ways,"
    declares the LORD.
 "As the heavens are higher than the earth,
  so are my ways higher than your ways
  and my thoughts than your thoughts.
As the rain and the snow
  come down from heaven,
and do not return to it
  without watering the earth
and making it bud and flourish,
  so that it yields seed for the sower and bread
  for the eater,
so is my word that goes out from my mouth:
  It will not return to me empty,
but will accomplish what I desire
  and achieve the purpose for which I sent it."

Isaiah 55:8–11

FRIDAY

Jesus said, "I am the Alpha and the Omega, the Beginning and the End. To him who is thirsty I will give to drink without cost from the spring of the water of life." ... Never again will they hunger; never again will they thirst. The sun will not beat upon them, nor any scorching heat. For the Lamb at the center of the throne will be their shepherd; he will lead them to springs of living water.

Revelation 21:6, 7:16–17

WEEKEND

The angel showed me the river of the water of life, as clear as crystal, flowing from the throne of God and of the Lamb down the middle of the great street of the city. On each side of the river stood the tree of life, bearing twelve crops of fruit, yielding its fruit every month. And the leaves of the tree are for the healing of the nations. No longer will there be any curse. The throne of God and of the Lamb will be in the city, and his servants will serve him. They will see his face, and his name will be on their foreheads. There will be no more night. They will not need the light of a lamp or the light of the sun, for the Lord God will give them light. And they will reign for ever and ever.

Revelation 22:1–5

MONDAY

In the beginning was the Word, and the Word
was with God, and the Word was God. The
Word became flesh and made his dwelling
among us. We have seen his glory, the glory of
the One and Only, who came from the Father,
full of grace and truth.

John 1:1, 14

Who has believed our message
    and to whom has the arm of the LORD been
    revealed?
He grew up before him like a tender shoot,
    and like a root out of dry ground.
He had no beauty or majesty to attract us to him,
    nothing in his appearance that we should
    desire him.
He was despised and rejected by men,
    a man of sorrows, and familiar with suffering.
Like one from whom men hide their faces
    he was despised, and we esteemed him not.

Isaiah 53:1–3

TUESDAY

Surely he took up our infirmities
    and carried our sorrows,
yet we considered him stricken by God,
    smitten by him, and afflicted.
But he was pierced for our transgressions,
    he was crushed for our iniquities;
the punishment that brought us peace was upon him,
    and by his wounds we are healed.

Isaiah 53:4–5

Christ came to that which was his own, but his
own did not receive him. Yet to all who received
him, to those who believed in his name, he gave
the right to become children of God—children
born not of natural descent, nor of human deci-
sion or a husband's will, but born of God.

John 1:11–13

WEDNESDAY

The people walking in darkness
    have seen a great light;
on those living in the land of the shadow of death
    a light has dawned. . . .
They rejoice before you
    as people rejoice at the harvest. . . .
For to us a child is born,
    to us a son is given,
    and the government will be on his shoulders.
And he will be called
    Wonderful Counselor, Mighty God,
    Everlasting Father, Prince of Peace.
Of the increase of his government and peace
    there will be no end.
He will reign on David's throne
    and over his kingdom,
establishing and upholding it
    with justice and righteousness
    from that time on and forever.

Isaiah 9:2–3, 6–7

THURSDAY

By his knowledge my righteous servant will
    justify many,
    and he will bear their iniquities.
Therefore I will give him a portion among
    the great,
    and he will divide the spoils with the strong,
because he poured out his life unto death,
    and was numbered with the transgressors.
For he bore the sin of many,
    and made intercession for the transgressors.

Isaiah 53:11–12

Christ was with God in the beginning. Through
him all things were made; without him nothing
was made that has been made. In him was life,
and that life was the light of men.

John 1:2–4

FRIDAY

The Spirit of the Sovereign LORD is on me,
    because the LORD has anointed me
    to preach good news to the poor.
He has sent me to bind up the brokenhearted,
    to proclaim freedom for the captives
    and release from darkness for the prisoners,
to proclaim the year of the LORD's favor
    and the day of vengeance of our God,
to comfort all who mourn,
    and provide for those who grieve in Zion—
to bestow on them a crown of beauty
    instead of ashes,
the oil of gladness
    instead of mourning,
and a garment of praise
    instead of a spirit of despair.
They will be called oaks of righteousness,
    a planting of the LORD
    for the display of his splendor.

Isaiah 61:1–3

WEEKEND

I saw heaven standing open and there before me was a white horse, whose rider is called Faithful and True. ... On his robe and on his thigh he has this name written: KING OF KINGS AND LORD OF LORDS. ... Then I saw a new heaven and a new earth, for the first heaven and the first earth had passed away, and there was no longer any sea. I saw the Holy City, the new Jerusalem, coming down out of heaven from God, prepared as a bride beautifully dressed for her husband. And I heard a loud voice from the throne saying, "Now the dwelling of God is with men, and he will live with them. They will be his people, and God himself will be with them and be their God. He will wipe every tear from their eyes. There will be no more death or mourning or crying or pain, for the old order of things has passed away."

Revelation 19:11, 16, 21:1–4

MONDAY

Blessed is he
    whose transgressions are forgiven,
    whose sins are covered.
Blessed is the man
    whose sin the LORD does not count against him
    and in whose spirit is no deceit. . . .
I acknowledged my sin to you
    and did not cover up my iniquity.
I said, "I will confess
    my transgressions to the LORD"—
and you forgave
    the guilt of my sin.

Psalm 32:1–2, 5

TUESDAY

"This is the covenant I will make with them after that time," says the Lord. "I will put my laws in their hearts, and I will write them on their minds. ... Their sins and lawless acts I will remember no more." And where these have been forgiven, there is no longer any sacrifice for sin. Therefore, ... since we have confidence to enter the Most Holy Place by the blood of Jesus, by a new and living way opened for us through the curtain, that is, his body, and since we have a great priest over the house of God, let us draw near to God with a sincere heart in full assurance of faith, having our hearts sprinkled to cleanse us from a guilty conscience and having our bodies washed with pure water.

Hebrews 10:16–22

WEDNESDAY

Have mercy on me, O God,
    according to your unfailing love;
according to your great compassion
    blot out my transgressions.
Wash away all my iniquity
    and cleanse me from my sin.
For I know my transgressions,
    and my sin is always before me.
Against you, you only, have I sinned
    and done what is evil in your sight,
so that you are proved right when you speak
    and justified when you judge.

Psalm 51:1–4

THURSDAY

Surely you desire truth in the inner parts;
  you teach me wisdom in the inmost place.
Cleanse me with hyssop, and I will be clean;
  wash me, and I will be whiter than snow.
Let me hear joy and gladness; . . .
Hide your face from my sins
  and blot out all my iniquity.
Create in me a pure heart, O God,
  and renew a steadfast spirit within me.

Psalm 51:6–10

If my people, who are called by my name, will
humble themselves and pray and seek my face
and turn from their wicked ways, then will I hear
from heaven and will forgive their sin and will
heal their land.

2 Chronicles 7:14

FRIDAY

We proclaim to you what we have seen and heard, so that you also may have fellowship with us. And our fellowship is with the Father and with his Son, Jesus Christ. We write this to make our joy complete. This is the message we have heard from him and declare to you: God is light; in him there is no darkness at all. … But if we walk in the light, as he is in the light, we have fellowship with one another, and the blood of Jesus, his Son, purifies us from all sin. If we claim to be without sin, we deceive ourselves and the truth is not in us. If we confess our sins, he is faithful and just and will forgive us our sins and purify us from all unrighteousness. … My dear children, I write this to you so that you will not sin. But if anybody does sin, we have one who speaks to the Father in our defense—Jesus Christ, the Righteous One.

1 John 1:3–5, 7–9, 2:1

WEEKEND

The LORD is compassionate and gracious,
    slow to anger, abounding in love.
He will not always accuse,
    nor will he harbor his anger forever;
he does not treat us as our sins deserve
    or repay us according to our iniquities.
For as high as the heavens are above the earth,
    so great is his love for those who fear him;
as far as the east is from the west,
    so far has he removed our transgressions from us.
As a father has compassion on his children,
    so the LORD has compassion on those who
    fear him;
for he knows how we are formed,
    he remembers that we are dust.

Psalm 103:8–14

MONDAY

Faith is being sure of what we hope for and certain of what we do not see. This is what the
ancients were commended for. By faith we
understand that the universe was formed at
God's command, so that what is seen was not
made out of what was visible. . . .
Without faith it is impossible to please God,
because anyone who comes to him must believe
that he exists and that he rewards those who
earnestly seek him.

Hebrews 11:1–3, 6

TUESDAY

By faith Abraham, when called to go to a place he would later receive as his inheritance, obeyed and went, even though he did not know where he was going. By faith Abraham made his home in the promised land like a stranger in a foreign country; he lived in tents, as did Isaac and Jacob, who were heirs with him of the same promise. For he was looking forward to the city with foundations, whose architect and builder is God. By faith Abraham, even though he was past age—and Sarah herself was barren—was enabled to become a father because he considered him faithful who had made the promise. And so from this one man, and he as good as dead, came descendants as numerous as the stars in the sky and as countless as the sand on the seashore.

Hebrews 11:8–12

WEDNESDAY

By faith Moses' parents hid him for three
months after he was born, because they saw he
was no ordinary child, and they were not afraid
of the king's edict.

By faith Moses, when he had grown up, refused
to be known as the son of Pharaoh's daughter.
He chose to be mistreated along with the people
of God rather than to enjoy the pleasures of sin
for a short time. He regarded disgrace for the
sake of Christ as of greater value than the treasures of Egypt, because he was looking ahead to
his reward.

By faith he left Egypt, not fearing the king's
anger; he persevered because he saw him who is
invisible. By faith he kept the Passover and the
sprinkling of blood, so that the destroyer of the
firstborn would not touch the firstborn of Israel.

Hebrews 11:23–28

THURSDAY

All these people were still living by faith when they died. They did not receive the things promised; they only saw them and welcomed them from a distance. And they admitted that they were aliens and strangers on earth.

People who say such things show that they are looking for a country of their own. If they had been thinking of the country they had left, they would have had opportunity to return. Instead, they were longing for a better country a heavenly one. Therefore God is not ashamed to be called their God, for he has prepared a city for them.

Hebrews 11:13–16

FRIDAY

It is by grace you have been saved, through faith—and this not from yourselves, it is the gift of God—not by works, so that no one can boast. For we are God's workmanship, created in Christ Jesus to do good works, which God prepared in advance for us to do.

Ephesians 2:8–10

If you confess with your mouth, "Jesus is Lord," and believe in your heart that God raised him from the dead, you will be saved. For it is with your heart that you believe and are justified, and it is with your mouth that you confess and are saved. As the Scripture says, "Anyone who trusts in him will never be put to shame."

Romans 10:9–11

WEEKEND

I do not have time to tell about Gideon, Barak,
Samson, Jephthah, David, Samuel and the
prophets, who through faith conquered king-
doms, administered justice, and gained what was
promised; who shut the mouths of lions,
quenched the fury of the flames, and escaped the
edge of the sword; whose weakness was turned to
strength; and who became powerful in battle and
routed foreign armies . . . the world was not worthy of them. . . .

Let us fix our eyes on Jesus, the author and per-
fecter of our faith, who for the joy set before him
endured the cross, scorning its shame, and sat
down at the right hand of the throne of God.

Hebrews 11:32–34, 38, 12:2

MONDAY

How lovely is your dwelling place,
    O LORD Almighty!
My soul yearns, even faints,
    for the courts of the LORD;
my heart and my flesh cry out
    for the living God.
Even the sparrow has found a home,
    and the swallow a nest for herself,
    where she may have her young—
a place near your altar,
    O LORD Almighty, my King and my God.
Blessed are those who dwell in your house;
    they are ever praising you.
Blessed are those whose strength is in you,
    who have set their hearts on pilgrimage.
As they pass through the Valley of Baca,
    they make it a place of springs;
    the autumn rains also cover it with pools.
They go from strength to strength,
    till each appears before God in Zion.

Psalm 84:1–7

TUESDAY

Ascribe to the LORD the glory due his name;
>   worship the LORD in the splendor of his holiness.
The voice of the LORD is over the waters;
>   the God of glory thunders,
>   the LORD thunders over the mighty waters.
The voice of the LORD is powerful;
>   the voice of the LORD is majestic. …
The voice of the LORD strikes
>   with flashes of lightning.
The voice of the LORD shakes the desert;
>   the LORD shakes the Desert of Kadesh.
The voice of the LORD twists the oaks
>   and strips the forests bare.
And in his temple all cry, "Glory!"
The LORD sits enthroned over the flood;
>   the LORD is enthroned as King forever.
The LORD gives strength to his people;
>   the LORD blesses his people with peace.

Psalm 29:2–4, 7–11

WEDNESDAY

My heart is steadfast, O God;
   I will sing and make music with all my soul.
Awake, harp and lyre!
   I will awaken the dawn.
I will praise you, O LORD, among the nations;
   I will sing of you among the peoples.
For great is your love, higher than the heavens;
   your faithfulness reaches to the skies.
Be exalted, O God, above the heavens,
   and let your glory be over all the earth.

Psalm 108:1–5

THURSDAY

The LORD is my strength and my song;
    he has become my salvation.
Shouts of joy and victory
    resound in the tents of the righteous:
"The LORD's right hand has done mighty things!
    The LORD's right hand is lifted high;
    the LORD's right hand has done mighty
    things!" ...
Open for me the gates of righteousness;
    I will enter and give thanks to the LORD. ...
I will give you thanks, for you answered me;
    you have become my salvation.
The stone the builders rejected
    has become the capstone;
the LORD has done this,
    and it is marvelous in our eyes.

Psalm 118:14–16, 19, 21–23

FRIDAY

This is the day the LORD has made;
 let us rejoice and be glad in it. . . .
Blessed is he who comes in the name of the LORD.
 From the house of the LORD we bless you.
The LORD is God,
 and he has made his light shine upon us.
With boughs in hand, join in the festal procession ...
You are my God, and I will give you thanks;
 you are my God, and I will exalt you.
Give thanks to the LORD, for he is good;
 his love endures forever.

Psalm 118:24, 26–29

WEEKEND

O LORD, our Lord,
    how majestic is your name in all the earth!
You have set your glory
    above the heavens.
From the lips of children and infants
    you have ordained praise
because of your enemies,
    to silence the foe and the avenger.
When I consider your heavens,
    the work of your fingers,
the moon and the stars,
    which you have set in place,
what is man that you are mindful of him,
    the son of man that you care for him?
You made him a little lower than the heavenly beings
    and crowned him with glory and honor.
You made him ruler over the works of your hands;
    you put everything under his feet:
all flocks and herds,
    and the beasts of the field,
the birds of the air,
    and the fish of the sea,
    all that swim the paths of the seas.
O LORD, our Lord,
    how majestic is your name in all the earth!

Psalm 8:1–9

MONDAY

In the beginning was the Word, and the Word
was with God, and the Word was God. He was
with God in the beginning. Through him all
things were made; without him nothing was
made that has been made. In him was life, and
that life was the light of men.

John 1:1–4

For the word of God is living and active. Sharper
than any double-edged sword, it penetrates even
to dividing soul and spirit, joints and marrow; it
judges the thoughts and attitudes of the heart.

Hebrews 4:12

TUESDAY

I have not departed from your laws, O LORD,
   for you yourself have taught me.
How sweet are your words to my taste,
   sweeter than honey to my mouth!
I gain understanding from your precepts;
   therefore I hate every wrong path.
Your word is a lamp to my feet
   and a light for my path.

Psalm 119:102–105

WEDNESDAY

How can a young man keep his way pure?
    By living according to your word.
I seek you with all my heart;
    do not let me stray from your commands.
I have hidden your word in my heart
    that I might not sin against you.
Praise be to you, O LORD;
    teach me your decrees.
With my lips I recount
    all the laws that come from your mouth.
I rejoice in following your statutes
    as one rejoices in great riches.
I meditate on your precepts
    and consider your ways.
I delight in your decrees;
    I will not neglect your word.

Psalm 119:9–16

THURSDAY

The statutes of the LORD are trustworthy,
    making wise the simple.
The precepts of the LORD are right,
    giving joy to the heart.
The commands of the LORD are radiant,
    giving light to the eyes.
The fear of the LORD is pure,
    enduring forever.
The ordinances of the LORD are sure
    and altogether righteous.
They are more precious than gold,
    than much pure gold;
they are sweeter than honey,
    than honey from the comb.
By them is your servant warned;
    in keeping them there is great reward.

Psalm 19:7–11

FRIDAY

If you accept my words
    and store up my commands within you,
turning your ear to wisdom
    and applying your heart to understanding,
and if you call out for insight
    and cry aloud for understanding,
and if you look for it as for silver
    and search for it as for hidden treasure,
then you will understand the fear of the LORD
    and find the knowledge of God.
For the LORD gives wisdom,
    and from his mouth come knowledge and
understanding.

Proverbs 2:1–6

WEEKEND

By the word of the LORD were the heavens made,
   their starry host by the breath of his mouth.
He gathers the waters of the sea into jars;
   he puts the deep into storehouses.
Let all the earth fear the LORD;
   let all the people of the world revere him.
For he spoke, and it came to be;
   he commanded, and it stood firm. ...
The plans of the LORD stand firm forever,
   the purposes of his heart through all
   generations.

Psalm 33:6–9, 11

MONDAY

Blessed is the man who finds wisdom,
    the man who gains understanding,
for she is more profitable than silver
    and yields better returns than gold.
She is more precious than rubies;
    nothing you desire can compare with her.
Long life is in her right hand;
    in her left hand are riches and honor.
Her ways are pleasant ways,
    and all her paths are peace.

Proverbs 3:13–17

TUESDAY

Do not forget my teaching,
    but keep my commands in your heart,
for they will prolong your life many years
    and bring you prosperity.
Let love and faithfulness never leave you;
    bind them around your neck,
    write them on the tablet of your heart.
Then you will win favor and a good name
    in the sight of God and man.
Trust in the LORD with all your heart
    and lean not on your own understanding;
in all your ways acknowledge him,
    and he will make your paths straight.

Proverbs 3:1–6

WEDNESDAY

Get wisdom, get understanding;
 do not forget my words or swerve from them.
Do not forsake wisdom, and she will protect you;
 love her, and she will watch over you.
Wisdom is supreme; therefore get wisdom.
 Though it cost all you have, get understanding.
Esteem her, and she will exalt you;
 embrace her, and she will honor you.
She will set a garland of grace on your head
 and present you with a crown of splendor.

Proverbs 4:5–9

THURSDAY

If any of you lacks wisdom, he should ask God,
who gives generously to all without finding fault,
and it will be given to him.

James 1:5

Continue in what you have learned and have
become convinced of, because you know those
from whom you learned it, and how from
infancy you have known the holy Scriptures,
which are able to make you wise for salvation
through faith in Christ Jesus. All Scripture is
God-breathed and is useful for teaching, rebuk-
ing, correcting and training in righteousness, so
that the man of God may be thoroughly
equipped for every good work.

2 Timothy 3:14–17

FRIDAY

Wisdom is a tree of life to those who embrace her;
  those who lay hold of her will be blessed.
By wisdom the LORD laid the earth's foundations,
  by understanding he set the heavens in place;
by his knowledge the deeps were divided,
  and the clouds let drop the dew. …
Preserve sound judgment and discernment,
  do not let them out of your sight;
they will be life for you,
  an ornament to grace your neck.
Then you will go on your way in safety,
  and your foot will not stumble;
when you lie down, you will not be afraid;
  when you lie down, your sleep will be sweet.

Proverbs 3:18–24

WEEKEND

Praise be to the name of God for ever and ever;
> wisdom and power are his.
He changes times and seasons;
> he sets up kings and deposes them.
He gives wisdom to the wise
> and knowledge to the discerning.
He reveals deep and hidden things;
> he knows what lies in darkness,
> and light dwells with him.

Daniel 2:20–22

MONDAY

He who unites himself with the Lord is one with him in spirit.

1 Corinthians 6:17

There is one body and one Spirit—just as you were called to one hope when you were called—one Lord, one faith, one baptism; one God and Father of all, who is over all and through all and in all.

Ephesians 4:4–6

I appeal to you, ... in the name of our Lord Jesus Christ, that all of you agree with one another so that there may be no divisions among you and that you may be perfectly united in mind and thought.

1 Corinthians 1:10

TUESDAY

It was God who gave some to be apostles, some to be prophets, some to be evangelists, and some to be pastors and teachers, to prepare God's people for works of service, so that the body of Christ may be built up until we all reach unity in the faith and in the knowledge of the Son of God and become mature, attaining to the whole measure of the fullness of Christ. ... Speaking the truth in love, we will in all things grow up into him who is the Head, that is, Christ. From him the whole body, joined and held together by every supporting ligament, grows and builds itself up in love, as each part does its work.

Ephesians 4:11–13, 15–16

WEDNESDAY

Jesus prayed, "My prayer is not that you take them out of the world but that you protect them from the evil one. They are not of the world, even as I am not of it. Sanctify them by the truth; your word is truth. As you sent me into the world, I have sent them into the world. For them I sanctify myself, that they too may be truly sanctified. My prayer is not for them alone. I pray also for those who will believe in me through their message, that all of them may be one, Father, just as you are in me and I am in you. May they also be in us so that the world may believe that you have sent me. I have given them the glory that you gave me, that they may be one as we are one: I in them and you in me. May they be brought to complete unity to let the world know that you sent me and have loved them even as you have loved me."

John 17:15–23

THURSDAY

There is neither Jew nor Greek, slave nor free,
male nor female, for you are all one in Christ
Jesus.

Galatians 3:28

May the God who gives endurance and encouragement give you a spirit of unity among yourselves as you follow Christ Jesus, so that with one
heart and mouth you may glorify the God and
Father of our Lord Jesus Christ. Accept one
another, then, just as Christ accepted you, in
order to bring praise to God

Romans 15:5–7

FRIDAY

How good and pleasant it is
  when brothers live together in unity!
It is like precious oil poured on the head,
  running down on the beard,
running down on Aaron's beard,
  down upon the collar of his robes.
It is as if the dew of Hermon
  were falling on Mount Zion.
For there the LORD bestows his blessing,
  even life forevermore.

Psalm 133:1–3

WEEKEND

We proclaim the Lord, admonishing and teaching everyone with all wisdom, so that we may present everyone perfect in Christ. To this end I labor, struggling with all his energy, which so powerfully works in me. . . . My purpose is that they may be encouraged in heart and united in love, so that they may have the full riches of complete understanding, in order that they may know the mystery of God, namely, Christ, in whom are hidden all the treasures of wisdom and knowledge.

Colossians 1:28—29, 2:2—3

MONDAY

From the fruit of his lips a man is filled with
     good things
         as surely as the work of his hands rewards him. ...
Reckless words pierce like a sword,
     but the tongue of the wise brings healing. ...
An anxious heart weighs a man down,
     but a kind word cheers him up.

Proverbs 12:14, 18, 25

TUESDAY

A man finds joy in giving an apt reply—
    and how good is a timely word!

Proverbs 15:23

A word aptly spoken
    is like apples of gold in settings of silver.
Like an earring of gold or an ornament of fine gold
    is a wise man's rebuke to a listening ear.
Like the coolness of snow at harvest time
    is a trustworthy messenger to those who send him;
    he refreshes the spirit of his masters.

Proverbs 25:11–13

WEDNESDAY

May the words of my mouth and the meditation
  of my heart
    be pleasing in your sight,
    O LORD, my Rock and my Redeemer.

Psalm 19:14

I will open my mouth in parables,
  I will utter hidden things, things from of old—
what we have heard and known,
  what our fathers have told us.
We will not hide them from their children;
  we will tell the next generation
the praiseworthy deeds of the LORD,
  his power, and the wonders he has done.

Psalm 78:2–4

THURSDAY

Is any one of you in trouble? He should pray. Is anyone happy? Let him sing songs of praise. Is any one of you sick? He should call the elders of the church to pray over him and anoint him with oil in the name of the Lord. And the prayer offered in faith will make the sick person well; the Lord will raise him up. If he has sinned, he will be forgiven. Therefore confess your sins to each other and pray for each other so that you may be healed. The prayer of a righteous man is powerful and effective.

James 5:13–16

FRIDAY

Speak to one another with psalms, hymns and
spiritual songs. Sing and make music in your
heart to the Lord, always giving thanks to God
the Father for everything, in the name of our
Lord Jesus Christ.

Ephesians 5:19–20

Let us consider how we may spur one another on
toward love and good deeds. Let us not give up
meeting together, as some are in the habit of
doing, but let us encourage one another—and all
the more as you see the Day approaching.

Hebrews 10:24–25

WEEKEND

Speaking the truth in love, we will in all things
grow up into him who is the Head, that is, Christ.

Ephesians 4:15

If anyone speaks, he should do it as one speaking
the very words of God. If anyone serves, he
should do it with the strength God provides, so
that in all things God may be praised through
Jesus Christ. To him be the glory and the power
for ever and ever. Amen.

1 Peter 4:11

MONDAY

Put on the full armor of God so that you can take your stand against the devil's schemes. For our struggle is not against flesh and blood, but against the rulers, against the authorities, against the powers of this dark world and against the spiritual forces of evil in the heavenly realms. Therefore put on the full armor of God, so that when the day of evil comes, you may be able to stand your ground, and after you have done everything, to stand.

Ephesians 6:11–13

TUESDAY

Stand firm then, with the belt of truth buckled around your waist, with the breastplate of right-eousness in place, and with your feet fitted with the readiness that comes from the gospel of peace. In addition to all this, take up the shield of faith, with which you can extinguish all the flaming arrows of the evil one. Take the helmet of salvation and the sword of the Spirit, which is the word of God.

Ephesians 6:14–17

WEDNESDAY

Praise the LORD, O my soul.
O LORD my God, you are very great;
 you are clothed with splendor and majesty.
He wraps himself in light as with a garment;
 he stretches out the heavens like a tent
 and lays the beams of his upper chambers on
 their waters.
He makes the clouds his chariot
 and rides on the wings of the wind.
He makes winds his messengers,
 flames of fire his servants.

Psalm 104:1–4

THURSDAY

Saul dressed David in his own tunic. He put a
coat of armor on him and a bronze helmet on his
head. David fastened on his sword over the tunic
and tried walking around, because he was not
used to them. "I cannot go in these," he said to
Saul, "because I am not used to them." So he
took them off. Then he took his staff in his
hand, chose five smooth stones from the stream,
put them in the pouch of his shepherd's bag and,
with his sling in his hand, approached the
Philistine. ... David said to the Philistine, "You
come against me with sword and spear and
javelin, but I come against you in the name of
the LORD Almighty, the God of the armies of
Israel, whom you have defied. This day the LORD
will hand you over to me, ... and the whole
world will know that there is a God in Israel."

1 Samuel 17:38–40, 45–46

FRIDAY

We do not belong to the night or to the darkness. So then, let us not be like others, who are asleep, but let us be alert and self-controlled. ... Since we belong to the day, let us be self-controlled, putting on faith and love as a breastplate, and the hope of salvation as a helmet. For God did not appoint us to suffer wrath but to receive salvation through our Lord Jesus Christ.

1 Thessalonians 5:5–6, 8–9

WEEKEND

O Sovereign LORD, my strong deliverer,
  who shields my head in the day of battle—
do not grant the wicked their desires, O LORD;
    do not let their plans succeed,
    or they will become proud. ...
I know that the LORD secures justice for the poor
    and upholds the cause of the needy.
Surely the righteous will praise your name
    and the upright will live before you.

Psalm 140:7–8, 12–13

MONDAY

Jesus said, "I am the good shepherd. The good shepherd lays down his life for the sheep. The hired hand is not the shepherd who owns the sheep. So when he sees the wolf coming, he abandons the sheep and runs away. Then the wolf attacks the flock and scatters it. The man runs away because he is a hired hand and cares nothing for the sheep. I am the good shepherd; I know my sheep and my sheep know me—just as the Father knows me and I know the Father—and I lay down my life for the sheep."

John 10:11–15

TUESDAY

The LORD tends his flock like a shepherd:
    He gathers the lambs in his arms
and carries them close to his heart;
    he gently leads those that have young.

Isaiah 40:11

The LORD is the strength of his people,
    a fortress of salvation for his anointed one.
Save your people and bless your inheritance;
    be their shepherd and carry them forever.

Psalm 28:8–9

WEDNESDAY

Jesus said, "The watchman opens the gate for the shepherd, and the sheep listen to his voice. He calls his own sheep by name and leads them out. When he has brought out all his own, he goes on ahead of them, and his sheep follow him because they know his voice. But they will never follow a stranger; in fact, they will run away from him because they do not recognize a stranger's voice. … I have other sheep that are not of this sheep pen. I must bring them also. They too will listen to my voice, and there shall be one flock and one shepherd."

John 10:3–5, 16

THURSDAY

Know that the LORD is God.
> It is he who made us, and we are his;
> > we are his people, the sheep of his pasture.

Enter his gates with thanksgiving
> and his courts with praise;
> > give thanks to him and praise his name.

For the LORD is good and his love endures forever;
> his faithfulness continues through all generations.

Psalm 100:3–5

FRIDAY

Jesus said, "My sheep listen to my voice; I know them, and they follow me. I give them eternal life, and they shall never perish; no one can snatch them out of my hand. My Father, who has given them to me, is greater than all; no one can snatch them out of my Father's hand."

John 10:27–29

May the God of peace, who through the blood of the eternal covenant brought back from the dead our Lord Jesus, that great Shepherd of the sheep, equip you with everything good for doing his will, and may he work in us what is pleasing to him, through Jesus Christ, to whom be glory for ever and ever. Amen.

Hebrews 13:20–21

WEEKEND

The LORD is my shepherd, I shall not be in want.
    He makes me lie down in green pastures,
he leads me beside quiet waters,
    he restores my soul.
He guides me in paths of righteousness
    for his name's sake.
Even though I walk
    through the valley of the shadow of death,
I will fear no evil,
    for you are with me;
your rod and your staff,
    they comfort me.
You prepare a table before me
    in the presence of my enemies.
You anoint my head with oil;
    my cup overflows.
Surely goodness and love will follow me
    all the days of my life,
and I will dwell in the house of the LORD
    forever.

Psalm 23

MONDAY

On one occasion an expert in the law stood up
to test Jesus. "Teacher," he asked, "what must I
do to inherit eternal life?"

"What is written in the Law?" he replied. "How
do you read it?"

He answered: " 'Love the Lord your God with all
your heart and with all your soul and with all
your strength and with all your mind'; and,
'Love your neighbor as yourself.' "

"You have answered correctly," Jesus replied. "Do
this and you will live."

Luke 10:25–28

TUESDAY

[An expert in the law] asked Jesus, "And who is my neighbor?"

In reply Jesus said: "A man was going down from Jerusalem to Jericho, when he fell into the hands of robbers. They stripped him of his clothes, beat him and went away, leaving him half dead. A priest happened to be going down the same road, and when he saw the man, he passed by on the other side. So too, a Levite, when he came to the place and saw him, passed by on the other side. But a Samaritan, as he traveled, came where the man was; and when he saw him, he took pity on him. The Samaritan went to him and bandaged his wounds, pouring on oil and wine. Then he put the man on his own donkey, took him to an inn and took care of him. . . . "Which of these three do you think was a neighbor to the man who fell into the hands of robbers?" The expert in the law replied, "The one who had mercy on him." Jesus told him, "Go and do likewise."

Luke 10:29–34, 36–37

WEDNESDAY

Jesus said, "My children, I will be with you only a little longer. You will look for me, and just as I told the Jews, so I tell you now: Where I am going, you cannot come.

"A new command I give you: Love one another. As I have loved you, so you must love one another. By this all men will know that you are my disciples, if you love one another."

John 13:33–35

THURSDAY

For the LORD your God is God of gods and Lord
of lords, the great God, mighty and awesome,
who shows no partiality and accepts no bribes.
He defends the cause of the fatherless and the
widow, and loves the alien, giving him food and
clothing. And you are to love those who are
aliens, for you yourselves were aliens in Egypt.

Deuteronomy 10:17–19

FRIDAY

As we have opportunity, let us do good to all people, especially to those who belong to the family of believers.

Galatians 6:10

Above all, love each other deeply, because love covers over a multitude of sins. Offer hospitality to one another without grumbling. Each one should use whatever gift he has received to serve others, faithfully administering God's grace in its various forms.

1 Peter 4:8–10

Confess your sins to each other and pray for each other so that you may be healed. The prayer of a righteous man is powerful and effective.

James 5:16

WEEKEND

Keep on loving each other as brothers. Do not forget to entertain strangers, for by so doing some people have entertained angels without knowing it. Remember those in prison as if you were their fellow prisoners, and those who are mistreated as if you yourselves were suffering.

Hebrews 13:1–3

Encourage one another and build each other up, just as in fact you are doing. … Live in peace with each other.

1 Thessalonians 5:11, 13

MONDAY

As Jesus and his disciples were on their way, he
came to a village where a woman named Martha
opened her home to him. She had a sister called
Mary, who sat at the Lord's feet listening to what
he said.

Luke 10:38–40

The Sovereign LORD wakens me
> morning by morning,
>> wakens my ear to listen like one being taught.

Isaiah 50:4

TUESDAY

Martha was distracted by all the preparations that
had to be made. She came to him and asked,
"Lord, don't you care that my sister has left me to
do the work by myself? Tell her to help me!"

Luke 10:40

"I desire mercy, not sacrifice," says the LORD,
"and acknowledgment of God rather than
burnt offerings."

Hosea 6:6

WEDNESDAY

"Martha, Martha," the Lord answered, "you are worried and upset about many things, but only one thing is needed. Mary has chosen what is better, and it will not be taken away from her."

Luke 10:41–42

Do not worry, saying, 'What shall we eat?' or 'What shall we drink?' or 'What shall we wear?' … But seek first God's kingdom and his righteousness, and all these things will be given to you as well.

Matthew 6:31, 33

THURSDAY

Now a man named Lazarus was sick. He was
from Bethany, the village of Mary and her sister
Martha. ... The sisters sent word to Jesus, "Lord,
the one you love is sick." When he heard this,
Jesus said, "This sickness will not end in death.
No, it is for God's glory so that God's Son may
be glorified through it." Jesus loved Martha and
her sister and Lazarus. Yet when he heard that
Lazarus was sick, he stayed where he was two
more days. ...[Then Jesus said to his disciples]
"Our friend Lazarus has fallen asleep; but I am
going [to Judea] to wake him up."

John 11:1, 3–6, 11

The sun has one kind of splendor, the moon
another and the stars another; and star differs
from star in splendor. So will it be with the resurrection of the dead. The body that is sown is
perishable, it is raised imperishable; it is sown in
dishonor, it is raised in glory; it is sown in weakness, it is raised in power.

1 Corinthians 15:41–43

FRIDAY

On his arrival [in Judea], Jesus found that Lazarus had already been in the tomb for four days. ... When Martha heard that Jesus was coming, she went out to meet him, but Mary stayed at home. "Lord," Martha said to Jesus, "if you had been here, my brother would not have died. But I know that even now God will give you whatever you ask."

Jesus said to her, "Your brother will rise again." Martha answered, "I know he will rise again in the resurrection at the last day." Jesus said to her, "I am the resurrection and the life. He who believes in me will live, even though he dies; and whoever lives and believes in me will never die. Do you believe this?"

"Yes, Lord," she told him, "I believe that you are the Christ, the Son of God, who was to come into the world."

John 11:17, 20–27

WEEKEND

Jesus ... came to the tomb. It was a cave with a stone laid across the entrance. "Take away the stone," he said.

"But, Lord," said Martha, the sister of the dead man, "by this time there is a bad odor, for he has been there four days."

Then Jesus said, "Did I not tell you that if you believed, you would see the glory of God?" So they took away the stone. Then Jesus looked up and said, "Father, I thank you that you have heard me. I knew that you always hear me, but I said this for the benefit of the people standing here, that they may believe that you sent me." When he had said this, Jesus called in a loud voice, "Lazarus, come out!" The dead man came out, his hands and feet wrapped with strips of linen, and a cloth around his face. Jesus said to them, "Take off the grave clothes and let him go." Therefore many of the Jews who had come to visit Mary, and had seen what Jesus did, put their faith in him.

John 11:38–45

MONDAY

One day Jesus was praying in a certain place. When he finished, one of his disciples said to him, "Lord, teach us to pray, just as John taught his disciples."

He said to them, "When you pray, say:

"'Father,

hallowed be your name,

your kingdom come.

Give us each day our daily bread.

Forgive us our sins,

for we also forgive everyone who sins against us.

And lead us not into temptation.'"

Luke 11:1–4

TUESDAY

Jesus said to them, "Suppose one of you has a friend, and he goes to him at midnight and says, 'Friend, lend me three loaves of bread, because a friend of mine on a journey has come to me, and I have nothing to set before him.'

"Then the one inside answers, 'Don't bother me. The door is already locked, and my children are with me in bed. I can't get up and give you anything.' I tell you, though he will not get up and give him the bread because he is his friend, yet because of the man's boldness he will get up and give him as much as he needs."

Luke 11:5–8

WEDNESDAY

Jesus said, "So I say to you: Ask and it will be given to you; seek and you will find; knock and the door will be opened to you. For everyone who asks receives; he who seeks finds; and to him who knocks, the door will be opened. "Which of you fathers, if your son asks for a fish, will give him a snake instead? Or if he asks for an egg, will give him a scorpion? If you then, though you are evil, know how to give good gifts to your children, how much more will your Father in heaven give the Holy Spirit to those who ask him!"

Luke 11:9–13

THURSDAY

Then Jesus told his disciples a parable to show
them that they should always pray and not give
up. He said: "In a certain town there was a judge
who neither feared God nor cared about men.
And there was a widow in that town who kept
coming to him with the plea, 'Grant me justice
against my adversary.'

"For some time he refused. But finally he said to
himself, 'Even though I don't fear God or care
about men, yet because this widow keeps bother-
ing me, I will see that she gets justice, so that she
won't eventually wear me out with her coming!'"
And the Lord said, "Listen to what the unjust
judge says. And will not God bring about justice
for his chosen ones, who cry out to him day and
night? Will he keep putting them off? I tell you,
he will see that they get justice, and quickly."

Luke 18:1–8

FRIDAY

Pray in the Spirit on all occasions with all kinds of prayers and requests. With this in mind, be alert and always keep on praying for all the saints.

Ephesians 6:18

Ever since I heard about your faith in the Lord Jesus and your love for all the saints, I have not stopped giving thanks for you, remembering you in my prayers.

Ephesians 1:15–16

The eyes of the Lord are on the righteous and his ears are attentive to their prayer.

1 Peter 3:12

WEEKEND

Be joyful always; pray continually; give thanks in
all circumstances, for this is God's will for you in
Christ Jesus.

1 Thessalonians 5:16–18

We always thank God for all of you, mentioning
you in our prayers. We continually remember before
our God and Father your work produced by faith,
your labor prompted by love, and your endurance
inspired by hope in our Lord Jesus Christ.

1 Thessalonians 1:2–3

Do not be anxious about anything, but in everything, by prayer and petition, with thanksgiving,
present your requests to God.

Philippians 4:6

MONDAY

He who dwells in the shelter of the Most High
> will rest in the shadow of the Almighty.
I will say of the LORD, "He is my refuge and my
> > fortress,
> my God, in whom I trust." ...
He will cover you with his feathers,
> and under his wings you will find refuge;
> his faithfulness will be your shield and
> > rampart.

Psalm 91:1–2, 4

TUESDAY

You will not fear the terror of night,
    nor the arrow that flies by day,
nor the pestilence that stalks in the darkness,
    nor the plague that destroys at midday.
A thousand may fall at your side,
    ten thousand at your right hand,
    but it will not come near you.
You will only observe with your eyes
    and see the punishment of the wicked.
If you make the Most High your dwelling—
    even the LORD, who is my refuge—
then no harm will befall you,
    no disaster will come near your tent.

Psalm 91:5–10

WEDNESDAY

The LORD will command his angels concerning you
    to guard you in all your ways;
they will lift you up in their hands,
    so that you will not strike your foot against
        a stone.
You will tread upon the lion and the cobra;
    you will trample the great lion and the serpent.
"Because he loves me," says the LORD, "I will
        rescue him;
    I will protect him, for he acknowledges
        my name.
He will call upon me, and I will answer him;
    I will be with him in trouble,
    I will deliver him and honor him.
With long life will I satisfy him
    and show him my salvation."

Psalm 91:11–16

THURSDAY

Let all who take refuge in you be glad, O LORD;
  let them ever sing for joy.
Spread your protection over them,
    that those who love your name may rejoice
      in you.
For surely, O LORD, you bless the righteous;
    you surround them with your favor as with
      a shield.

Psalm 5:11–12

Jesus prayed, "Holy Father, protect [my disciples]
by the power of your name—the name you gave
me—so that they may be one as we are one.
While I was with them, I protected them and
kept them safe by that name you gave me."

John 17:11–12

FRIDAY

Find rest, O my soul, in God alone;
    my hope comes from him.
He alone is my rock and my salvation;
    he is my fortress, I will not be shaken.
My salvation and my honor depend on God;
    he is my mighty rock, my refuge.
Trust in him at all times, O people;
    pour out your hearts to him,
    for God is our refuge.

Psalm 62:5–8

WEEKEND

The LORD protects the simple hearted;
    When I was in great need, he saved me.
Be at rest once more, O my soul,
    for the LORD has been good to you.

Psalm 116:6–7

To him who is able to keep you from falling and
to present you before his glorious presence without fault and with great joy—to the only God
our Savior be glory, majesty, power and authority, through Jesus Christ our Lord, before all
ages, now and forevermore! Amen.

Jude 24–25

MONDAY

The angel said... "Do not be afraid, Zechariah;
your prayer has been heard. Your wife Elizabeth
will bear you a son, and you are to give him the
name John. He will be a joy and delight to you,
and many will rejoice because of his birth, for he
will be great in the sight of the Lord. He is never
to take wine or other fermented drink, and he
will be filled with the Holy Spirit even from
birth. Many of the people of Israel will he bring
back to the Lord their God. And he will go on
before the Lord, in the spirit and power of
Elijah, to turn the hearts of the fathers to their
children and the disobedient to the wisdom of
the righteous—to make ready a people prepared
for the Lord."

Luke 1:13–17

TUESDAY

In the fifteenth year of the reign of Tiberius
Caesar . . . during the high priesthood of Annas
and Caiaphas, the word of God came to John
son of Zechariah in the desert. He went into all
the country around the Jordan, preaching a baptism of repentance for the forgiveness of sins.

Luke 3:1–3

You who bring good tidings to Zion,
  go up on a high mountain.
You who bring good tidings to Jerusalem,
  lift up your voice with a shout,
lift it up, do not be afraid;
  say to the towns of Judah,
  "Here is your God!"

Isaiah 40:9

WEDNESDAY

A voice of one calling:
"In the desert prepare
   the way for the LORD;
make straight in the wilderness
   a highway for our God.
Every valley shall be raised up,
   every mountain and hill made low;
the rough ground shall become level,
   the rugged places a plain.
And the glory of the LORD will be revealed,
   and all mankind together will see it.
   For the mouth of the LORD has spoken."

Isaiah 40:3–5

THURSDAY

The people were waiting expectantly and were all wondering in their hearts if John might possibly be the Christ.

John answered them all, "I baptize you with water. But one more powerful than I will come, the thongs of whose sandals I am not worthy to untie. He will baptize you with the Holy Spirit and with fire."

Luke 3:15–16

When the day of Pentecost came, [the believers] were all together in one place. Suddenly a sound like the blowing of a violent wind came from heaven and filled the whole house where they were sitting. They saw what seemed to be tongues of fire that separated and came to rest on each of them. All of them were filled with the Holy Spirit and began to speak in other tongues as the Spirit enabled them.

Acts 2:1–4

FRIDAY

Then Jesus came from Galilee to the Jordan to be baptized by John. But John tried to deter him, saying, "I need to be baptized by you, and do you come to me?"

Jesus replied, "Let it be so now; it is proper for us to do this to fulfill all righteousness." Then John consented.

As soon as Jesus was baptized, he went up out of the water. At that moment heaven was opened, and he saw the Spirit of God descending like a dove and lighting on him. And a voice from heaven said, "This is my Son, whom I love; with him I am well pleased."

Matthew 3:13–17

WEEKEND

The next day John saw Jesus coming toward him
and said, "Look, the Lamb of God, who takes
away the sin of the world! This is the one I
meant when I said, 'A man who comes after me
has surpassed me because he was before me.' I
myself did not know him, but the reason I came
baptizing with water was that he might be
revealed to Israel."

Then John gave this testimony: "I saw the Spirit
come down from heaven as a dove and remain
on him. I would not have known him, except
that the one who sent me to baptize with water
told me, 'The man on whom you see the Spirit
come down and remain is he who will baptize
with the Holy Spirit.' I have seen and I testify
that this is the Son of God."

John 1:29–34

MONDAY

If only for this life we have hope in Christ, we
are to be pitied more than all men. But Christ
has indeed been raised from the dead, the firstfruits of those who have fallen asleep.

For since death came through a man, the resurrection of the dead comes also through a man.
For as in Adam all die, so in Christ all will be
made alive. But each in his own turn: Christ, the
firstfruits; then, when he comes, those who
belong to him.

Then the end will come, when he hands over the
kingdom to God the Father after he has
destroyed all dominion, authority and power.
For he must reign until he has put all his enemies under his feet. The last enemy to be
destroyed is death.

1 Corinthians 15:19–26

TUESDAY

We were therefore buried with him through baptism into death in order that, just as Christ was raised from the dead through the glory of the Father, we too may live a new life. If we have been united with him like this in his death, we will certainly also be united with him in his resurrection. For we know that our old self was crucified with him so that the body of sin might be done away with, that we should no longer be slaves to sin—because anyone who has died has been freed from sin. Now if we died with Christ, we believe that we will also live with him. For we know that since Christ was raised from the dead, he cannot die again; death no longer has mastery over him. The death he died, he died to sin once for all; but the life he lives, he lives to God. In the same way, count yourselves dead to sin but alive to God in Christ Jesus.

Romans 6:4–11

WEDNESDAY

Someone may ask, "How are the dead raised?
With what kind of body will they come?" ...
All flesh is not the same: Men have one kind of
flesh, animals have another, birds another and
fish another. There are also heavenly bodies and
there are earthly bodies; but the splendor of the
heavenly bodies is one kind, and the splendor of
the earthly bodies is another.
The sun has one kind of splendor, the moon
another and the stars another; and star differs
from star in splendor. So will it be with the resurrection of the dead. The body that is sown is
perishable, it is raised imperishable; it is sown in
dishonor, it is raised in glory; it is sown in weakness, it is raised in power; it is sown a natural
body, it is raised a spiritual body. If there is a natural body, there is also a spiritual body.

1 Corinthians 15:35, 39–44

THURSDAY

As was the earthly man, so are those who are of
the earth; and as is the man from heaven, so also
are those who are of heaven. And just as we have
borne the likeness of the earthly man, so shall we
bear the likeness of the man from heaven. I
declare to you, brothers, that flesh and blood
cannot inherit the kingdom of God, nor does the
perishable inherit the imperishable.

Listen, I tell you a mystery: We will not all sleep,
but we will all be changed—in a flash, in the
twinkling of an eye, at the last trumpet. For the
trumpet will sound, the dead will be raised
imperishable, and we will be changed. For the
perishable must clothe itself with the imperishable, and the mortal with immortality.

1 Corinthians 15:48–53

FRIDAY

When the perishable has been clothed with the
imperishable, and the mortal with immortality,
then the saying that is written will come true:
"Death has been swallowed up in victory."
"Where, O death, is your victory? Where, O
death, is your sting?"
The sting of death is sin, and the power of sin is
the law. But thanks be to God! He gives us the
victory through our Lord Jesus Christ.
Therefore, my dear brothers, stand firm. Let
nothing move you.

1 Corinthians 15:54–58

WEEKEND

I saw a new heaven and a new earth, for the first
heaven and the first earth had passed away, and
there was no longer any sea. I saw the Holy City,
the new Jerusalem, coming down out of heaven
from God, prepared as a bride beautifully dressed
for her husband. And I heard a loud voice from
the throne saying, "Now the dwelling of God is
with men, and he will live with them. They will be
his people, and God himself will be with them and
be their God. He will wipe every tear from their
eyes. There will be no more death or mourning or
crying or pain, for the old order of things has
passed away."

He who was seated on the throne said, "I am making everything new!" Then he said, "Write this
down, for these words are trustworthy and true."

Revelation 21:1–5

MONDAY

This is what the LORD Almighty says: "Here is the man whose name is the Branch, and he will branch out from his place and build the temple of the LORD. It is he who will build the temple of the LORD, and he will be clothed with majesty and will sit and rule on his throne. And he will be a priest on his throne. And there will be harmony between the two."

Zechariah 6:12–13

Since we have a great high priest who has gone through the heavens, Jesus the Son of God, let us hold firmly to the faith we profess.

Hebrews 4:14

TUESDAY

We do not have a high priest who is unable to
sympathize with our weaknesses, but we have
one who has been tempted in every way, just as
we are—yet was without sin. Let us then
approach the throne of grace with confidence, so
that we may receive mercy and find grace to help
us in our time of need.

Hebrews 4:15–16

This is the confidence we have in approaching
God: that if we ask anything according to his
will, he hears us.

1 John 5:14

WEDNESDAY

Since the children have flesh and blood, he too
shared in their humanity so that by his death
he might destroy him who holds the power of
death ... For this reason he had to be made like
his brothers in every way, in order that he might
become a merciful and faithful high priest in service to God, and that he might make atonement
for the sins of the people. Because he himself suffered when he was tempted, he is able to help
those who are being tempted. Therefore, holy
brothers, who share in the heavenly calling, fix
your thoughts on Jesus, the apostle and high priest
whom we confess.

Hebrews 2:14, 17—3:1

THURSDAY

Because Jesus lives forever, he has a permanent
priesthood. Therefore he is able to save com-
pletely those who come to God through him,
because he always lives to intercede for them.
Such a high priest meets our need—one who is
holy, blameless, pure, set apart from sinners,
exalted above the heavens. Unlike the other high
priests, he does not need to offer sacrifices day
after day, first for his own sins, and then for the
sins of the people. He sacrificed for their sins
once for all when he offered himself.

Hebrews 7:24–27

FRIDAY

During the days of Jesus' life on earth, he offered up prayers and petitions with loud cries and tears to the one who could save him from death, and he was heard because of his reverent submission. Although he was a son, he learned obedience from what he suffered and, once made perfect, he became the source of eternal salvation for all who obey him and was designated by God to be high priest in the order of Melchizedek. . . . This Melchizedek was king of Salem and priest of God Most High. He met Abraham returning from the defeat of the kings and blessed him, and Abraham gave him a tenth of everything. First, his name means "king of righteousness"; then also, "king of Salem" means "king of peace." Without father or mother, without genealogy, without beginning of days or end of life, like the Son of God he remains a priest forever.

Hebrews 5:7–10, 7:1–3

WEEKEND

When Christ came as high priest of the good
things that are already here, he went through the
greater and more perfect tabernacle that is not
man-made, that is to say, not a part of this creation. He did not enter by means of the blood of
goats and calves; but he entered the Most Holy
Place once for all by his own blood, having
obtained eternal redemption. The blood of goats
and bulls and the ashes of a heifer sprinkled on
those who are ceremonially unclean sanctify them
so that they are outwardly clean. How much
more, then, will the blood of Christ, who through
the eternal Spirit offered himself unblemished to
God, cleanse our consciences from acts that lead
to death, so that we may serve the living God! For
this reason Christ is the mediator of a new
covenant, that those who are called may receive
the promised eternal inheritance—now that he
has died as a ransom to set them free from the sins
committed under the first covenant.

Hebrews 9:11–15

MONDAY

Now there was a man of the Pharisees named
Nicodemus, a member of the Jewish ruling
council. He came to Jesus at night and said,
"Rabbi, we know you are a teacher who has
come from God. For no one could perform the
miraculous signs you are doing if God were not
with him."
In reply Jesus declared, "I tell you the truth, no
one can see the kingdom of God unless he is
born again."

John 3:1–3

TUESDAY

"How can a man be born when he is old?"
Nicodemus asked. "Surely he cannot enter a second time into his mother's womb to be born!"
Jesus answered, "I tell you the truth, no one can
enter the kingdom of God unless he is born of
water and the Spirit. Flesh gives birth to flesh,
but the Spirit gives birth to spirit. You should
not be surprised at my saying, 'You must be born
again.'"

John 3:4–7

WEDNESDAY

"The wind blows wherever it pleases. You hear its sound, but you cannot tell where it comes from or where it is going. So it is with everyone born of the Spirit."

"How can this be?" Nicodemus asked.

"You are Israel's teacher," said Jesus, "and do you not understand these things? I tell you the truth, we speak of what we know, and we testify to what we have seen, but still you people do not accept our testimony. I have spoken to you of earthly things and you do not believe; how then will you believe if I speak of heavenly things?"

John 3:8–12

THURSDAY

Jesus told Nicodemus, "No one has ever gone into heaven except the one who came from heaven—the Son of Man. Just as Moses lifted up the snake in the desert, so the Son of Man must be lifted up, that everyone who believes in him may have eternal life.

"For God so loved the world that he gave his one and only Son, that whoever believes in him shall not perish but have eternal life."

John 3:13–16

FRIDAY

Jesus said to Nicodemus, "God did not send his
Son into the world to condemn the world, but to
save the world through him. Whoever believes in
him is not condemned, but whoever does not
believe stands condemned already because he
has not believed in the name of God's one and
only Son.

"This is the verdict: Light has come into the
world, but men loved darkness instead of light
because their deeds were evil. Everyone who does
evil hates the light, and will not come into the
light for fear that his deeds will be exposed. But
whoever lives by the truth comes into the light,
so that it may be seen plainly that what he has
done has been done through God."

John 3:17–21

WEEKEND

If you confess with your mouth, "Jesus is Lord," and believe in your heart that God raised him from the dead, you will be saved. For it is with your heart that you believe and are justified, and it is with your mouth that you confess and are saved. As the Scripture says, "Anyone who trusts in him will never be put to shame."

Romans 10:9–11

Though you have not seen Christ, you love him; and even though you do not see him now, you believe in him and are filled with an inexpressible and glorious joy, for you are receiving the goal of your faith, the salvation of your souls.

1 Peter 1:8–9

MONDAY

I lift up my eyes to the hills—
  where does my help come from?
My help comes from the LORD,
  the Maker of heaven and earth.
He will not let your foot slip—
  he who watches over you will not slumber.
indeed, he who watches over Israel
  will neither slumber nor sleep

Psalm 121:1–4

TUESDAY

The LORD watches over you—
    the LORD is your shade at your right hand;
the sun will not harm you by day,
    nor the moon by night.
The LORD will keep you from all harm—
    he will watch over your life;
the LORD will watch over your coming and
      going
    both now and forevermore.

Psalm 121:5–8

WEDNESDAY

Those who trust in the LORD are like Mount Zion,
    which cannot be shaken but endures forever.
As the mountains surround Jerusalem,
    so the LORD surrounds his people
    both now and forevermore.
The scepter of the wicked will not remain
    over the land allotted to the righteous,
for then the righteous might use
    their hands to do evil.
Do good, O LORD, to those who are good,
    to those who are upright in heart.
But those who turn to crooked ways
    the LORD will banish with the evildoers.

Psalm 125:1–5

THURSDAY

When the LORD brought back the captives to Zion,
    we were like men who dreamed.
Our mouths were filled with laughter,
    our tongues with songs of joy.
Then it was said among the nations,
    "The LORD has done great things for them."
The LORD has done great things for us,
    and we are filled with joy.
Restore our fortunes, O LORD,
    like streams in the Negev.
Those who sow in tears
    will reap with songs of joy.
He who goes out weeping,
    carrying seed to sow,
will return with songs of joy,
    carrying sheaves with him.

Psalm 126:1–6

FRIDAY

Unless the LORD builds the house,
  its builders labor in vain.
Unless the LORD watches over the city,
  the watchmen stand guard in vain.
In vain you rise early
  and stay up late,
toiling for food to eat—
  for he grants sleep to those he loves.
Sons are a heritage from the LORD,
  children a reward from him.
Like arrows in the hands of a warrior
  are sons born in one's youth.
Blessed is the man
  whose quiver is full of them.
They will not be put to shame. . . .

Psalm 127:1–5

WEEKEND

Blessed are all who fear the LORD,
  who walk in his ways.
You will eat the fruit of your labor;
  blessings and prosperity will be yours.
Your wife will be like a fruitful vine
  within your house;
your sons will be like olive shoots
  around your table.
Thus is the man blessed
  who fears the LORD.
May the LORD bless you from Zion
  all the days of your life;
may you see the prosperity of Jerusalem,
  and may you live to see your children's children.

Psalm 128:1–6

MONDAY

Now a man came up to Jesus and asked, "Teacher, what good thing must I do to get eternal life?"

"Why do you ask me about what is good?" Jesus replied. "There is only One who is good. If you want to enter life, obey the commandments."

"Which ones?" the man inquired. Jesus replied, "'Do not murder, do not commit adultery, do not steal, do not give false testimony, honor your father and mother,' and 'love your neighbor as yourself.'"

"All I have kept," the young man said. "What do I still lack?"

Jesus answered, "If you want to be perfect, go, sell your possessions and give to the poor, and you will have treasure in heaven. Then come, follow me."

When the young man heard this, he went away sad, because he had great wealth.

Matthew 19:16–22

TUESDAY

Jesus said to his disciples, "I tell you the truth, it is hard for a rich man to enter the kingdom of heaven. Again I tell you, it is easier for a camel to go through the eye of a needle than for a rich man to enter the kingdom of God."

When the disciples heard this, they were greatly astonished and asked, "Who then can be saved?"

Jesus looked at them and said, "With man this is impossible, but with God all things are possible."

Peter answered him, "We have left everything to follow you! What then will there be for us?"

Jesus said to them, "I tell you the truth, at the renewal of all things, when the Son of Man sits on his glorious throne, you who have followed me will also sit on twelve thrones, judging the twelve tribes of Israel. And everyone who has left houses or brothers or sisters or father or mother or children or fields for my sake will receive a hundred times as much and will inherit eternal life."

Matthew 19:23–29

WEDNESDAY

Jesus said, "Do not store up for yourselves treasures on earth, where moth and rust destroy, and where thieves break in and steal. But store up for yourselves treasures in heaven, where moth and rust do not destroy, and where thieves do not break in and steal. For where your treasure is, there your heart will be also."

Matthew 6:19–21

"Behold, I am coming soon!," says the Lord Jesus. "My reward is with me, and I will give to everyone according to what he has done."

Revelation 22:12

THURSDAY

My God will meet all your needs according to
his glorious riches in Christ Jesus.

Philippians 4:19

I pray that out of God's glorious riches he may
strengthen you with power through his Spirit in
your inner being, so that Christ may dwell in
your hearts through faith. And I pray that you,
being rooted and established in love, may have
power, together with all the saints, to grasp how
wide and long and high and deep is the love of
Christ, and to know this love that surpasses
knowledge—that you may be filled to the measure of all the fullness of God.

Ephesians 3:16–19

FRIDAY

I keep asking that the God of our Lord Jesus
Christ, the glorious Father, may give you the
Spirit of wisdom and revelation, so that you may
know him better. I pray also that the eyes of your
heart may be enlightened in order that you may
know the hope to which he has called you, the
riches of his glorious inheritance in the saints,
and his incomparably great power for us who
believe. That power is like the working of his
mighty strength, which he exerted in Christ
when he raised him from the dead and seated
him at his right hand in the heavenly realms, far
above all rule and authority, power and dominion, and every title that can be given, not only in
the present age but also in the one to come. And
God placed all things under his feet and
appointed him to be head over everything for the
church, which is his body, the fullness of him
who fills everything in every way.

Ephesians 1:17–23

WEEKEND

Because of his great love for us, God, who is rich
in mercy, made us alive with Christ even when
we were dead in transgressions—it is by grace
you have been saved. And God raised us up with
Christ and seated us with him in the heavenly
realms in Christ Jesus, in order that in the coming ages he might show the incomparable riches
of his grace, expressed in his kindness to us in
Christ Jesus.

Ephesians 2:4–7

MONDAY

The people rejoiced at the willing response of
their leaders, for they had given freely and
wholeheartedly to the LORD. David the king also
rejoiced greatly. David praised the LORD in the
presence of the whole assembly, saying, . . .
"Yours, O LORD, is the greatness and the power
    and the glory and the majesty and the splendor,
    for everything in heaven and earth is yours.
Yours, O LORD, is the kingdom;
    you are exalted as head over all.
Wealth and honor come from you;
    you are the ruler of all things.
In your hands are strength and power
    to exalt and give strength to all.
Now, our God, we give you thanks,
    and praise your glorious name.
"But who am I, and who are my people, that we
should be able to give as generously as this?
Everything comes from you, and we have given
you only what comes from your hand."

1 Chronicles 29:9–14

TUESDAY

The righteous give generously; ...
If the LORD delights in a man's way,
    he makes his steps firm;
though he stumble, he will not fall,
    for the LORD upholds him with his hand.
I was young and now I am old,
        yet I have never seen the righteous forsaken
        or their children begging bread.
They are always generous and lend freely;
        their children will be blessed. ...
For the LORD loves the just
        and will not forsake his faithful ones.
They will be protected forever ...
        the righteous will inherit the land
        and dwell in it forever.

Psalm 37:21, 23–26, 28–29

WEDNESDAY

When you give to the needy, do not announce it
with trumpets, as the hypocrites do in the synagogues and on the streets, to be honored by men.
I tell you the truth, they have received their
reward in full. But when you give to the needy,
do not let your left hand know what your right
hand is doing, so that your giving may be in
secret. Then your Father, who sees what is done
in secret, will reward you.

Matthew 6:2–4

THURSDAY

Freely you have received, freely give.

Matthew 10:8

Remember this: Whoever sows sparingly will
also reap sparingly, and whoever sows generously
will also reap generously. Each man should give
what he has decided in his heart to give, not
reluctantly or under compulsion, for God loves a
cheerful giver.

2 Corinthians 9:6–7

FRIDAY

God is able to make all grace abound to you, so
that in all things at all times, having all that you
need, you will abound in every good work. As it
is written: "He has scattered abroad his gifts to
the poor; his righteousness endures forever."
Now he who supplies seed to the sower and
bread for food will also supply and increase your
store of seed and will enlarge the harvest of your
righteousness. You will be made rich in every
way so that you can be generous on every occasion, and through us your generosity will result
in thanksgiving to God.

2 Corinthians 9:8–11

WEEKEND

This service that you perform is not only supplying the needs of God's people but is also overflowing in many expressions of thanks to God. Because of the service by which you have proved yourselves, men will praise God for the obedience that accompanies your confession of the gospel of Christ, and for your generosity in sharing with them and with everyone else. And in their prayers for you their hearts will go out to you, because of the surpassing grace God has given you.

2 Corinthians 9:12–14

MONDAY

Jesus said, "Your Father knows what you need
before you ask him.
"This, then, is how you should pray:

   "'Our Father in heaven,
hallowed be your name,
your kingdom come,
your will be done
    on earth as it is in heaven.
Give us today our daily bread.
Forgive us our debts,
    as we also have forgiven our debtors.
And lead us not into temptation,
but deliver us from the evil one.'"

Matthew 6:8–13

TUESDAY

When you pray, do not be like the hypocrites,
for they love to pray standing in the synagogues
and on the street corners to be seen by men. I
tell you the truth, they have received their reward
in full. But when you pray, go into your room,
close the door and pray to your Father, who is
unseen. Then your Father, who sees what is done
in secret, will reward you.

Matthew 6:5–6

WEDNESDAY

Early in the morning, as he was on his way back
to the city, Jesus was hungry. Seeing a fig tree by
the road, he went up to it but found nothing on
it except leaves. Then he said to it, "May you
never bear fruit again!" Immediately the tree
withered.

When the disciples saw this, they were amazed.
"How did the fig tree wither so quickly?" they
asked.

Jesus replied, "I tell you the truth, if you have
faith and do not doubt, not only can you do
what was done to the fig tree, but also you can
say to this mountain, 'Go, throw yourself into
the sea,' and it will be done. If you believe, you
will receive whatever you ask for in prayer."

Matthew 21:18–22

THURSDAY

Jesus said, "I tell you the truth, my Father will give you whatever you ask in my name. Until now you have not asked for anything in my name. Ask and you will receive, and your joy will be complete."

John 16:23–24

The LORD has heard my cry for mercy;
    the LORD accepts my prayer.

Psalm 6:9

God has surely listened
    and heard my voice in prayer.
Praise be to God,
    who has not rejected my prayer
    or withheld his love from me!

Psalm 66:19–20

FRIDAY

Is any one of you in trouble? He should pray. Is anyone happy? Let him sing songs of praise. Is any one of you sick? He should call the elders of the church to pray over him and anoint him with oil in the name of the Lord. And the prayer offered in faith will make the sick person well; the Lord will raise him up. If he has sinned, he will be forgiven. Therefore confess your sins to each other and pray for each other so that you may be healed. The prayer of a righteous man is powerful and effective.

James 5:13–16

WEEKEND

Jesus prayed, "[Father,] I pray for [my disciples]. I am not praying for the world, but for those you have given me, for they are yours. … I will remain in the world no longer, but they are still in the world, and I am coming to you. Holy Father, protect them by the power of your name—the name you gave me—so that they may be one as we are one. … My prayer is not for them alone. I pray also for those who will believe in me through their message, that all of them may be one, Father, just as you are in me and I am in you. May they also be in us so that the world may believe that you have sent me. I have given them the glory that you gave me, that they may be one as we are one: I in them and you in me. May they be brought to complete unity to let the world know that you sent me and have loved them even as you have loved me."

John 17:9, 11, 20–23

MONDAY

Sing to him, sing praise to him;
  tell of all his wonderful acts.
Glory in his holy name;
  let the hearts of those who seek the LORD rejoice.
Look to the Lord and his strength;
  seek his face always.

1 Chronicles 16:9–11

Stand up and praise the LORD your God, who is from everlasting to everlasting. Blessed be your glorious name, and may it be exalted above all blessing and praise. You alone are the LORD. You made the heavens, even the highest heavens, and all their starry host, the earth and all that is on it, the seas and all that is in them. You give life to everything, and the multitudes of heaven worship you.

Nehemiah 9:5–6

TUESDAY

The LORD is compassionate and gracious,
  slow to anger, abounding in love.
He will not always accuse,
  nor will he harbor his anger forever;
he does not treat us as our sins deserve
  or repay us according to our iniquities.
For as high as the heavens are above the earth,
  so great is his love for those who fear him;
as far as the east is from the west,
  so far has he removed our transgressions from us.

Psalm 103:8–12

WEDNESDAY

As a father has compassion on his children,
    so the LORD has compassion on those who
        fear him;
for he knows how we are formed,
    he remembers that we are dust.
But from everlasting to everlasting
    the LORD's love is with those who fear him,
    and his righteousness with their children's
        children—
with those who keep his covenant
    and remember to obey his precepts.

Psalm 103:13–14, 17–18

THURSDAY

The LORD has established his throne in heaven,
    and his kingdom rules over all.
Praise the LORD, you his angels,
    you mighty ones who do his bidding,
    who obey his word.
Praise the LORD, all his heavenly hosts,
    you his servants who do his will.
Praise the LORD, all his works
    everywhere in his dominion.
Praise the LORD, O my soul.

Psalm 103:19–22

FRIDAY

My heart is steadfast, O God;
  I will sing and make music with all my soul.
Awake, harp and lyre!
  I will awaken the dawn.
I will praise you, O LORD, among the nations;
  I will sing of you among the peoples.
For great is your love, higher than the heavens;
  your faithfulness reaches to the skies.
Be exalted, O God, above the heavens,
  and let your glory be over all the earth.

Psalm 108:1–5

WEEKEND

Sing to the LORD, praise his name;
    proclaim his salvation day after day.
Declare his glory among the nations,
    his marvelous deeds among all peoples.
For great is the LORD and most worthy of praise;
    he is to be feared above all gods. …
Splendor and majesty are before him;
    strength and glory are in his sanctuary.
Ascribe to the LORD, O families of nations,
    ascribe to the LORD glory and strength.
Ascribe to the LORD the glory due his name;
    bring an offering and come into his courts.
Worship the LORD in the splendor of his holiness;
    tremble before him, all the earth.

Psalm 96:2–4, 6–9

MONDAY

This is how we know that we love the children of
God: by loving God and carrying out his commands. This is love for God: to obey his commands. And his commands are not burdensome,
for everyone born of God overcomes the world.
This is the victory that has overcome the world,
even our faith. Who is it that overcomes the
world? Only he who believes that Jesus is the
Son of God.

1 John 5:2–5

TUESDAY

Jesus said, "Since you have kept my command to endure patiently, I will also keep you ... I am coming soon. Hold on to what you have, so that no one will take your crown. Him who over-comes I will make a pillar in the temple of my God. Never again will he leave it. I will write on him the name of my God and the name of the city of my God, the new Jerusalem, which is coming down out of heaven from my God; and I will also write on him my new name."

Revelation 3:10–12

WEDNESDAY

Jesus said, "I have told you these things, so that in me you may have peace. In this world you will have trouble. But take heart! I have overcome the world."

John 16:33

You, dear children, are from God and have overcome [false prophets], because the one who is in you is greater than the one who is in the world.

1 John 4:4

If your enemy is hungry, feed him; if he is thirsty, give him something to drink. . . . Do not be overcome by evil, but overcome evil with good.

Romans 12:20–21

THURSDAY

Jesus said, "Here I am! I stand at the door and knock. If anyone hears my voice and opens the door, I will come in and eat with him, and he with me. To him who overcomes, I will give the right to sit with me on my throne, just as I overcame and sat down with my Father on his throne. He who has an ear, let him hear what the Spirit says to the churches."

Revelation 3:20–22

FRIDAY

To him who overcomes, I will give the right to eat from the tree of life, which is in the paradise of God.

To him who overcomes and does my will to the end, I will give authority over the nations—'He will rule them with an iron scepter; he will dash them to pieces like pottery'—just as I have received authority from my Father. I will also give him the morning star. . . .

He who overcomes will, like them, be dressed in white. I will never blot out his name from the book of life, but will acknowledge his name before my Father and his angels.

Revelation 2:7, 26–28, 3:5

WEEKEND

I heard a loud voice from the throne saying,
"Now the dwelling of God is with men, and he
will live with them. They will be his people, and
God himself will be with them and be their God.
He will wipe every tear from their eyes. There
will be no more death or mourning or crying or
pain, for the old order of things has passed
away."

He who was seated on the throne said, "I am
making everything new!" Then he said, "Write
this down, for these words are trustworthy and
true."

He said to me: "It is done. I am the Alpha and
the Omega, the Beginning and the End. To him
who is thirsty I will give to drink without cost
from the spring of the water of life. He who
overcomes will inherit all this, and I will be his
God and he will be my son."

Revelation 21:3–7

MONDAY

Everything that was written in the past was written to teach us, so that through endurance and the encouragement of the Scriptures we might have hope. May the God who gives endurance and encouragement give you a spirit of unity among yourselves as you follow Christ Jesus, so that with one heart and mouth you may glorify the God and Father of our Lord Jesus Christ.

Romans 15:4–6

TUESDAY

We always thank God for all of you, mentioning you in our prayers. We continually remember before our God and Father your work produced by faith, your labor prompted by love, and your endurance inspired by hope in our Lord Jesus Christ.

1 Thessalonians 1:2–3

Fight the good fight of the faith. Take hold of the eternal life to which you were called when you made your good confession in the presence of many witnesses.

1 Timothy 6:12

WEDNESDAY

Since the day we heard about you, we have not stopped praying for you and asking God to fill you with the knowledge of his will through all spiritual wisdom and understanding. And we pray this in order that you may live a life worthy of the Lord and may please him in every way: bearing fruit in every good work, growing in the knowledge of God, being strengthened with all power according to his glorious might so that you may have great endurance and patience, and joyfully giving thanks to the Father, who has qualified you to share in the inheritance of the saints in the kingdom of light.

Colossians 1:9–12

THURSDAY

Endure hardship with us like a good soldier of Christ Jesus. No one serving as a soldier gets involved in civilian affairs—he wants to please his commanding officer. Similarly, if anyone competes as an athlete, he does not receive the victor's crown unless he competes according to the rules. The hardworking farmer should be the first to receive a share of the crops. Reflect on what I am saying, for the Lord will give you insight into all this.

2 Timothy 2:3–7

FRIDAY

I always thank God for you because of his grace given you in Christ Jesus. For in him you have been enriched in every way—in all your speaking and in all your knowledge—because our testimony about Christ was confirmed in you. Therefore you do not lack any spiritual gift as you eagerly wait for our Lord Jesus Christ to be revealed. He will keep you strong to the end, so that you will be blameless on the day of our Lord Jesus Christ. God, who has called you into fellowship with his Son Jesus Christ our Lord, is faithful.

1 Corinthians 1:4–9

WEEKEND

Jesus said, "Since you have kept my command to endure patiently, I will also keep you from the hour of trial that is going to come upon the whole world to test those who live on the earth. I am coming soon. Hold on to what you have, so that no one will take your crown.

Him who overcomes I will make a pillar in the temple of my God. Never again will he leave it. I will write on him the name of my God and the name of the city of my God, the new Jerusalem, which is coming down out of heaven from my God; and I will also write on him my new name."

Revelation 3:10–12

MONDAY

O LORD, you have searched me
    and you know me.
You know when I sit and when I rise;
    you perceive my thoughts from afar.
You discern my going out and my lying down;
    you are familiar with all my ways.
Before a word is on my tongue
    you know it completely, O LORD.

Psalm 139:1–4

TUESDAY

You hem me in—behind and before, LORD;
  you have laid your hand upon me.
Such knowledge is too wonderful for me,
  too lofty for me to attain.
Where can I go from your Spirit?
  Where can I flee from your presence?
If I go up to the heavens, you are there;
  if I make my bed in the depths, you are there.

Psalm 139:5–8

WEDNESDAY

If I rise on the wings of the dawn,
　　if I settle on the far side of the sea,
even there your hand will guide me,
　　your right hand will hold me fast.
If I say, "Surely the darkness will hide me
　　and the light become night around me,"
even the darkness will not be dark to you;
　　the night will shine like the day,
　　for darkness is as light to you.

Psalm 139:9–12

THURSDAY

For you created my inmost being;
> you knit me together in my mother's womb.
I praise you because I am fearfully and
> > wonderfully made;
> your works are wonderful,
> > I know that full well.
My frame was not hidden from you
> when I was made in the secret place.
When I was woven together in the depths of
> > the earth,
> your eyes saw my unformed body.
All the days ordained for me
> were written in your book
before one of them came to be.

Psalm 139:13–16

FRIDAY

Jesus said, "I will ask the Father, and he will give you another Counselor to be with you forever— the Spirit of truth. The world cannot accept him, because it neither sees him nor knows him. But you know him, for he lives with you and will be in you. I will not leave you as orphans; I will come to you.

"Before long, the world will not see me anymore, but you will see me. Because I live, you also will live. On that day you will realize that I am in my Father, and you are in me, and I am in you. Whoever has my commands and obeys them, he is the one who loves me. He who loves me will be loved by my Father, and I too will love him and show myself to him."

John 14:16–21

WEEKEND

Jesus said, "The Counselor, the Holy Spirit, whom the Father will send in my name, will teach you all things and will remind you of everything I have said to you. Peace I leave with you; my peace I give you. I do not give to you as the world gives. Do not let your hearts be troubled and do not be afraid."

John 14:26–27

Jesus came to [the disciples] and said, "All authority in heaven and on earth has been given to me. Therefore go and make disciples of all nations, baptizing them in the name of the Father and of the Son and of the Holy Spirit, and teaching them to obey everything I have commanded you. And surely I am with you always, to the very end of the age."

Matthew 28:18–20

MONDAY

When Abram was ninety-nine years old, the
LORD appeared to him and said, "I am God
Almighty; walk before me and be blameless. I
will confirm my covenant between me and you
and will greatly increase your numbers."
Abram fell facedown, and God said to him, "As
for me, this is my covenant with you: You will be
the father of many nations. No longer will you
be called Abram; your name will be Abraham,
for I have made you a father of many nations. I
will make you very fruitful; I will make nations
of you, and kings will come from you. I will
establish my covenant as an everlasting covenant
between me and you and your descendants after
you for the generations to come, to be your God
and the God of your descendants after you."

Genesis 17:1–7

TUESDAY

God tested Abraham. He said to him, ...
"Take your son, your only son, Isaac, whom you
love, and go to the region of Moriah. Sacrifice
him there as a burnt offering on one of the
mountains I will tell you about."
Early the next morning Abraham got up and
saddled his donkey. He took with him two of his
servants and his son Isaac. When he had cut
enough wood for the burnt offering, he set out
for the place God had told him about. ...
Abraham took the wood for the burnt offering
and placed it on his son Isaac, and he himself
carried the fire and the knife. As the two of them
went on together, Isaac spoke up and said to his
father Abraham, "Father?"
"Yes, my son?" Abraham replied.
"The fire and wood are here," Isaac said, "but
where is the lamb for the burnt offering?"
Abraham answered, "God himself will provide
the lamb for the burnt offering, my son." And
the two of them went on together.

Genesis 22:1–3, 6–8

WEDNESDAY

When they reached the place God had told him
about, Abraham built an altar there and arranged
the wood on it. He bound his son Isaac and laid
him on the altar, on top of the wood. Then he
reached out his hand and took the knife to slay
his son. But the angel of the LORD called out to
him from heaven, "Abraham! Abraham!"

"Here I am," he replied.

"Do not lay a hand on the boy," he said. "Do
not do anything to him. Now I know that you
fear God, because you have not withheld from
me your son, your only son."

Abraham looked up and there in a thicket he saw
a ram caught by its horns. He went over and
took the ram and sacrificed it as a burnt offering
instead of his son. So Abraham called that place
The LORD Will Provide. And to this day it is
said, "On the mountain of the LORD it will be
provided."

Genesis 22:9–14

THURSDAY

The angel of the LORD called to Abraham from
heaven a second time and said, "I swear by
myself, declares the LORD, that because you have
done this and have not withheld your son, your
only son, I will surely bless you and make your
descendants as numerous as the stars in the sky
and as the sand on the seashore. Your descendants will take possession of the cities of their
enemies, and through your offspring all nations
on earth will be blessed, because you have
obeyed me."

Genesis 22:15–18

FRIDAY

"The time is coming, declares the Lord, when I will make a new covenant with the house of Israel and with the house of Judah. It will not be like the covenant I made with their forefathers when I took them by the hand to lead them out of Egypt, because they did not remain faithful to my covenant, and I turned away from them, declares the Lord. This is the covenant I will make with the house of Israel after that time, declares the Lord. I will put my laws in their minds and write them on their hearts. I will be their God, and they will be my people. No longer will a man teach his neighbor, or a man his brother, saying, 'Know the Lord,' because they will all know me, from the least of them to the greatest. For I will forgive their wickedness and will remember their sins no more."

Hebrews 8:8–12

WEEKEND

Jesus took the cup, gave thanks and offered it to
them, saying, "Drink from it, all of you. This is
my blood of the covenant, which is poured out
for many for the forgiveness of sins."

Matthew 26:27–28

We are not like Moses, who would put a veil
over his face to keep the Israelites from gazing at
it while the radiance was fading away. But their
minds were made dull, for to this day the same
veil remains when the old covenant is read. It has
not been removed, because only in Christ is it
taken away. Even to this day when Moses is read,
a veil covers their hearts.
But whenever anyone turns to the Lord, the veil
is taken away. Now the Lord is the Spirit, and
where the Spirit of the Lord is, there is freedom.
And we, who with unveiled faces all reflect the
Lord's glory, are being transformed into his likeness with ever-increasing glory, which comes
from the Lord, who is the Spirit.

2 Corinthians 3:13–18

MONDAY

Christ is the mediator of a new covenant, that
those who are called may receive the promised
eternal inheritance—now that he has died as a
ransom to set them free from the sins committed
under the first covenant. ... For Christ did not
enter a man-made sanctuary that was only a
copy of the true one; he entered heaven itself,
now to appear for us in God's presence. Nor did
he enter heaven to offer himself again and again,
the way the high priest enters the Most Holy
Place every year with blood that is not his own.
Then Christ would have had to suffer many
times since the creation of the world. But now he
has appeared once for all at the end of the ages to
do away with sin by the sacrifice of himself.

Hebrews 9:15, 24–26

TUESDAY

There is one God and one mediator between God and men, the man Christ Jesus, who gave himself as a ransom for all men—the testimony given in its proper time.

1 Timothy 2:5–6

The Spirit helps us in our weakness. We do not know what we ought to pray for, but the Spirit himself intercedes for us with groans that words cannot express. And he who searches our hearts knows the mind of the Spirit, because the Spirit intercedes for the saints in accordance with God's will.

Romans 8:26–27

WEDNESDAY

For those God foreknew he also predestined to
be conformed to the likeness of his Son, that he
might be the firstborn among many brothers.
And those he predestined, he also called; those
he called, he also justified; those he justified, he
also glorified.

What, then, shall we say in response to this? If
God is for us, who can be against us? He who
did not spare his own Son, but gave him up for
us all—how will he not also, along with him,
graciously give us all things?

Who will bring any charge against those whom
God has chosen? It is God who justifies.

Who is he that condemns? Christ Jesus, who
died—more than that, who was raised to life—is
at the right hand of God and is also interceding
for us.

Romans 8:29–34

THURSDAY

[The Messiah] was pierced for our transgressions,
   he was crushed for our iniquities;
the punishment that brought us peace was upon him,
   and by his wounds we are healed.
We all, like sheep, have gone astray,
   each of us has turned to his own way;
and the LORD has laid on him
   the iniquity of us all.

Isaiah 53:5–6

FRIDAY

After the suffering of his soul,
　　[The Messiah] will see the light of life and be
　　　satisfied;
by his knowledge my righteous servant will
　　　justify many,
　　and he will bear their iniquities.
Therefore I will give him a portion among
　　　the great,
　　and he will divide the spoils with the strong,
because he poured out his life unto death,
　　and was numbered with the transgressors.
For he bore the sin of many,
　　and made intercession for the transgressors.

Isaiah 53:11–12

WEEKEND

Even now my witness is in heaven;
    my advocate is on high.
My intercessor is my friend
    as my eyes pour out tears to God;
on behalf of a man he pleads with God
    as a man pleads for his friend.

Job 16:19–21

If anybody does sin, we have one who speaks to the Father in our defense—Jesus Christ, the Righteous One. He is the atoning sacrifice for our sins, and not only for ours but also for the sins of the whole world.

1 John 2:1–2

MONDAY

There is no difference between Jew and
Gentile—the same Lord is Lord of all and richly
blesses all who call on him, for, "Everyone who
calls on the name of the Lord will be saved."
How, then, can they call on the one they have
not believed in? And how can they believe in the
one of whom they have not heard? And how can
they hear without someone preaching to them?
And how can they preach unless they are sent?
As it is written, "How beautiful are the feet of
those who bring good news!" . . .
Faith comes from hearing the message, and the
message is heard through the word of Christ.

Romans 10:12–15, 17

TUESDAY

Jesus came to [his disciples] and said, "All
authority in heaven and on earth has been given
to me. Therefore go and make disciples of all
nations, baptizing them in the name of the
Father and of the Son and of the Holy Spirit,
and teaching them to obey everything I have
commanded you. And surely I am with you
always, to the very end of the age."

Matthew 28:18–19

WEDNESDAY

Paul said, "As I came near Damascus, suddenly a
bright light from heaven flashed around me. I
fell to the ground and heard a voice say to me,
'Saul! Saul! Why do you persecute me?'

"'Who are you, Lord?' I asked.

"'I am Jesus of Nazareth, whom you are perse-
cuting,' he replied. . . .

"'What shall I do, Lord?' I asked.

"'Get up,' the Lord said, "and go into Damascus.
There you will be told all that you have been
assigned to do.'"

"My companions led me by the hand into
Damascus, because the brilliance of the light had
blinded me. A man named Ananias came to see
me. . . . He stood beside me and said, 'Brother
Saul, receive your sight!' And at that very
moment I was able to see him. Then he said:
'The God of our fathers has chosen you to know
his will and to see the Righteous One and to hear
words from his mouth. You will be his witness to
all men of what you have seen and heard.'"

Acts 22:6–8, 10–15

THURSDAY

I am not ashamed of the gospel, because it is the
power of God for the salvation of everyone who
believes. ... For in the gospel a righteousness
from God is revealed, a righteousness that is by
faith from first to last, just as it is written: "The
righteous will live by faith."

Romans 1:16–17

I will praise you, O LORD, with all my heart;
  I will tell of all your wonders.

Psalm 9:1

FRIDAY

The Spirit of the Sovereign LORD is on me,
   because the LORD has anointed me
   to preach good news to the poor.
He has sent me to bind up the brokenhearted,
   to proclaim freedom for the captives
   and release from darkness for the prisoners,
to proclaim the year of the LORD's favor
   and the day of vengeance of our God,
to comfort all who mourn,
   and provide for those who grieve in Zion—
to bestow on them a crown of beauty
   instead of ashes,
the oil of gladness
   instead of mourning,
and a garment of praise
   instead of a spirit of despair.
They will be called oaks of righteousness,
   a planting of the LORD
for the display of his splendor.

Isaiah 61:1–3

WEEKEND

"Is not this the kind of fasting I have chosen:
to loose the chains of injustice
    and untie the cords of the yoke,
to set the oppressed free
    and break every yoke?
Is it not to share your food with the hungry
    and to provide the poor wanderer with shelter—
when you see the naked, to clothe him,
    and not to turn away from your own flesh
and blood?
Then your light will break forth like the dawn,
    and your healing will quickly appear;
then your righteousness will go before you,
    and the glory of the LORD will be your rear
guard,"
declares the LORD.

Isaiah 58:6–8

MONDAY

Now I will show you the most excellent way. If I speak in the tongues of men and of angels, but have not love, I am only a resounding gong or a clanging cymbal. If I have the gift of prophecy and can fathom all mysteries and all knowledge, and if I have a faith that can move mountains, but have not love, I am nothing. If I give all I possess to the poor and surrender my body to the flames, but have not love, I gain nothing.

1 Corinthians 12:31—13:3

TUESDAY

Love is patient, love is kind. It does not envy, it does not boast, it is not proud. It is not rude, it is not self-seeking, it is not easily angered, it keeps no record of wrongs. Love does not delight in evil but rejoices with the truth. It always protects, always trusts, always hopes, always perseveres. Love never fails.

1 Corinthians 13:4–8

WEDNESDAY

And now these three remain: faith, hope and love. But the greatest of these is love.

1 Corinthians 13:13

In Christ Jesus . . . the only thing that counts is faith expressing itself through love.

Galatians 5:6

We know and rely on the love God has for us. God is love. Whoever lives in love lives in God, and God in him.

1 John 4:16

. In your unfailing love, O LORD, you will lead
   the people you have redeemed.
In your strength you will guide them
   to your holy dwelling.

Exodus 15:13

THURSDAY

How great is the love the Father has lavished on us, that we should be called children of God! And that is what we are! ... This is how we know what love is: Jesus Christ laid down his life for us. And we ought to lay down our lives for our brothers. ... Dear children, let us not love with words or tongue but with actions and in truth.

1 John 3:1, 16, 18

FRIDAY

Dear friends, let us love one another, for love comes from God. Everyone who loves has been born of God and knows God. Whoever does not love does not know God, because God is love. This is how God showed his love among us: He sent his one and only Son into the world that we might live through him. This is love: not that we loved God, but that he loved us and sent his Son as an atoning sacrifice for our sins. Dear friends, since God so loved us, we also ought to love one another. No one has ever seen God; but if we love one another, God lives in us and his love is made complete in us.

1 John 4:7–12

WEEKEND

We know that we live in God and he in us,
because he has given us of his Spirit. And we have
seen and testify that the Father has sent his Son
to be the Savior of the world. If anyone acknowl-
edges that Jesus is the Son of God, God lives in
him and he in God. ... In this way, love is made
complete among us so that we will have confidence on the day of judgment, because in this
world we are like him. There is no fear in love.
But perfect love drives out fear, because fear has
to do with punishment. ... We love because he
first loved us.

1 John 4:13–15, 17–19

MONDAY

The LORD will yet fill your mouth with laughter
and your lips with shouts of joy.

Job 8:21

You have made known to me the path of life,
O LORD;
you will fill me with joy in your presence,
with eternal pleasures at your right hand.

Psalm 16:11

The LORD is my strength and my shield;
my heart trusts in him, and I am helped.
My heart leaps for joy
and I will give thanks to him in song.

Psalm 28:7

TUESDAY

Those living far away fear your wonders, O LORD;
    where morning dawns and evening fades
    you call forth songs of joy.
You care for the land and water it;
    you enrich it abundantly.
The streams of God are filled with water
    to provide the people with grain,
    for so you have ordained it.
You drench its furrows
    and level its ridges;
you soften it with showers
    and bless its crops.
You crown the year with your bounty,
    and your carts overflow with abundance.
The grasslands of the desert overflow;
    the hills are clothed with gladness.
The meadows are covered with flocks
    and the valleys are mantled with grain;
they shout for joy and sing.

Psalm 65:8–13

WEDNESDAY

Shout with joy to God, all the earth!
　　Sing the glory of his name;
　　make his praise glorious!
Say to God, "How awesome are your deeds!
　　So great is your power
　　that your enemies cringe before you.
All the earth bows down to you;
　　they sing praise to you,
　　they sing praise to your name."
Come and see what God has done,
　　how awesome his works in man's behalf!

Psalm 66:1–5

THURSDAY

Jesus said, "As the Father has loved me, so have I loved you. Now remain in my love. If you obey my commands, you will remain in my love, just as I have obeyed my Father's commands and remain in his love. I have told you this so that my joy may be in you and that your joy may be complete."

John 15:9–11

May the God of hope fill you with all joy and peace as you trust in him, so that you may overflow with hope by the power of the Holy Spirit.

Romans 15:13

FRIDAY

Tremble before him, all the earth!
 The world is firmly established; it cannot be
  moved.
Let the heavens rejoice, let the earth be glad;
 let them say among the nations, "The LORD
  reigns!"
Let the sea resound, and all that is in it;
 let the fields be jubilant, and everything in
  them!
Then the trees of the forest will sing,
 they will sing for joy before the LORD,
 for he comes to judge the earth.
Give thanks to the LORD, for he is good;
 his love endures forever.

1 Chronicles 16:30–34

WEEKEND

The ransomed of the LORD will return.
They will enter Zion with singing;
    everlasting joy will crown their heads.
Gladness and joy will overtake them,
    and sorrow and sighing will flee away.

Isaiah 35:10

The joy of the LORD is your strength.

Nehemiah 8:10

The LORD has done great things for us,
    and we are filled with joy.

Psalm 126:3

MONDAY

Jesus looked toward heaven and prayed: "Father, the time has come. Glorify your Son, that your Son may glorify you. For you granted him authority over all people that he might give eternal life to all those you have given him. Now this is eternal life: that they may know you, the only true God, and Jesus Christ, whom you have sent."

John 17:1–3

TUESDAY

Jesus prayed, "I have brought you glory on earth
by completing the work you gave me to do. And
now, Father, glorify me in your presence with the
glory I had with you before the world began.
I have revealed you to those whom you gave me
out of the world. They were yours; you gave
them to me and they have obeyed your word.
Now they know that everything you have given
me comes from you. For I gave them the words
you gave me and they accepted them. They knew
with certainty that I came from you, and they
believed that you sent me."

John 17:4–8

WEDNESDAY

Jesus prayed, "I am not praying for the world, but for those you have given me, for they are yours. All I have is yours, and all you have is mine. And glory has come to me through them. I will remain in the world no longer, but they are still in the world, and I am coming to you. Holy Father, protect them by the power of your name—the name you gave me—so that they may be one as we are one. While I was with them, I protected them and kept them safe by that name you gave me. None has been lost except the one doomed to destruction so that Scripture would be fulfilled.

I am coming to you now, but I say these things while I am still in the world, so that they may have the full measure of my joy within them."

John 17:9–13

THURSDAY

Jesus prayed, "I have given them your word and the world has hated them, for they are not of the world any more than I am of the world. My prayer is not that you take them out of the world but that you protect them from the evil one. They are not of the world, even as I am not of it. Sanctify them by the truth; your word is truth."

John 17:14–17

FRIDAY

Jesus prayed, "As you sent me into the world, I have sent them into the world. For them I sanctify myself, that they too may be truly sanctified. My prayer is not for them alone. I pray also for those who will believe in me through their message, that all of them may be one, Father, just as you are in me and I am in you. May they also be in us so that the world may believe that you have sent me. I have given them the glory that you gave me, that they may be one as we are one: I in them and you in me."

John 17:18–23

WEEKEND

Jesus prayed, "May they be brought to complete
unity to let the world know that you sent me
and have loved them even as you have loved me.
"Father, I want those you have given me to be
with me where I am, and to see my glory, the
glory you have given me because you loved me
before the creation of the world.
"Righteous Father, though the world does not
know you, I know you, and they know that you
have sent me. I have made you known to them,
and will continue to make you known in order
that the love you have for me may be in them
and that I myself may be in them."

John 17:23–26

MONDAY

It was just before the Passover Feast. Jesus knew
that the time had come for him to leave this
world and go to the Father. Having loved his
own who were in the world, he now showed
them the full extent of his love. ... Jesus knew
that the Father had put all things under his
power, and that he had come from God and was
returning to God. Jesus got up from the meal,
took off his outer clothing, and wrapped a towel
around his waist. After that, he poured water
into a basin and began to wash his disciples' feet,
drying them with the towel that was wrapped
around him.

Jesus came to Simon Peter, who said to him,
"Lord, are you going to wash my feet?"

Jesus replied, "You do not realize now what I am
doing, but later you will understand."

"No," said Peter, "you shall never wash my feet."

Jesus answered, "Unless I wash you, you have no
part with me."

"Then, Lord," Simon Peter replied, "not just my
feet but my hands and my head as well!"

John 13:1, 3–9

TUESDAY

When Jesus had finished washing their feet, he put on his clothes and returned to his place. "Do you understand what I have done for you?" he asked them.

"You call me 'Teacher' and 'Lord,' and rightly so, for that is what I am. Now that I, your Lord and Teacher, have washed your feet, you also should wash one another's feet. I have set you an example that you should do as I have done for you. "I tell you the truth, no servant is greater than his master, nor is a messenger greater than the one who sent him. Now that you know these things, you will be blessed if you do them."

John 13:12–17

WEDNESDAY

Good and upright is the LORD; . . .
He guides the humble in what is right
  and teaches them his way.
All the ways of the LORD are loving and faithful
  for those who keep the demands of his
    covenant.

Psalm 25:8–10

Humble yourselves before the Lord, and he will
lift you up.

James 4:10

As God's chosen people, holy and dearly loved,
clothe yourselves with compassion, kindness,
humility, gentleness and patience.

Colossians 3:12

THURSDAY

Do nothing out of selfish ambition or vain conceit, but in humility consider others better than yourselves. ... Your attitude should be the same as that of Christ Jesus:
Who, being in very nature God,
    did not consider equality with God something
        to be grasped,
but made himself nothing,
    taking the very nature of a servant,
    being made in human likeness.
And being found in appearance as a man,
    he humbled himself
    and became obedient to death—
        even death on a cross!
Therefore God exalted him to the highest place
    and gave him the name that is above every
        name,
that at the name of Jesus every knee should bow,
    in heaven and on earth and under the earth,
and every tongue confess that Jesus Christ is Lord,
    to the glory of God the Father.

Philippians 2:3, 5–11

FRIDAY

To some who were confident of their own righteousness and looked down on everybody else,
Jesus told this parable: "Two men went up to the
temple to pray, one a Pharisee and the other a tax
collector. The Pharisee stood up and prayed
about himself: 'God, I thank you that I am not
like other men—robbers, evildoers, adulterers—
or even like this tax collector. I fast twice a week
and give a tenth of all I get.'
"But the tax collector stood at a distance. He
would not even look up to heaven, but beat his
breast and said, 'God, have mercy on me, a sinner.'
"I tell you that this man, rather than the other,
went home justified before God. For everyone
who exalts himself will be humbled, and he who
humbles himself will be exalted."

Luke 18:9–14

WEEKEND

People were ... bringing babies to Jesus to have him touch them. When the disciples saw this, they rebuked them. But Jesus called the children to him and said, "Let the little children come to me, and do not hinder them, for the kingdom of God belongs to such as these. I tell you the truth, anyone who will not receive the kingdom of God like a little child will never enter it."

Luke 18:15–17

The disciples came to Jesus and asked, "Who is the greatest in the kingdom of heaven?"
He called a little child and had him stand among them. And he said: "I tell you the truth, unless you change and become like little children, you will never enter the kingdom of heaven. Therefore, whoever humbles himself like this child is the greatest in the kingdom of heaven."

Matthew 18:1–4

MONDAY

Jesus said, "When the Counselor comes, whom I will send to you from the Father, the Spirit of truth who goes out from the Father, he will testify about me. And you also must testify, for you have been with me from the beginning." . . . "But I tell you the truth: It is for your good that I am going away. Unless I go away, the Counselor will not come to you; but if I go, I will send him to you."

John 15:26–27—16:7

"When he, the Spirit of truth, comes, he will guide you into all truth. He will not speak on his own; he will speak only what he hears, and he will tell you what is yet to come. He will bring glory to me by taking from what is mine and making it known to you. All that belongs to the Father is mine. That is why I said the Spirit will take from what is mine and make it known to you."

John 16:13–15

TUESDAY

There is now no condemnation for those who
are in Christ Jesus, because through Christ Jesus
the law of the Spirit of life set me free from the
law of sin and death.

For what the law was powerless to do in that it
was weakened by the sinful nature, God did by
sending his own Son in the likeness of sinful
man to be a sin offering. And so he condemned
sin in sinful man, in order that the righteous
requirements of the law might be fully met in us,
who do not live according to the sinful nature
but according to the Spirit.

Romans 8:1–4

WEDNESDAY

Those who live according to the sinful nature
have their minds set on what that nature desires;
but those who live in accordance with the Spirit
have their minds set on what the Spirit desires.
The mind of sinful man is death, but the mind
controlled by the Spirit is life and peace; the sinful mind is hostile to God. It does not submit to
God's law, nor can it do so. Those controlled by
the sinful nature cannot please God.
You, however, are controlled not by the sinful
nature but by the Spirit, if the Spirit of God lives
in you. And if anyone does not have the Spirit of
Christ, he does not belong to Christ.

Romans 8:5–9

THURSDAY

If Christ is in you, your body is dead because of sin, yet your spirit is alive because of righteousness. And if the Spirit of him who raised Jesus from the dead is living in you, he who raised Christ from the dead will also give life to your mortal bodies through his Spirit, who lives in you. Therefore, brothers, we have an obligation—but it is not to the sinful nature, to live according to it. For if you live according to the sinful nature, you will die; but if by the Spirit you put to death the misdeeds of the body, you will live, because those who are led by the Spirit of God are sons of God.

Romans 8:10–14

FRIDAY

You did not receive a spirit that makes you a slave again to fear, but you received the Spirit of sonship. And by him we cry, "*Abba*, Father." The Spirit himself testifies with our spirit that we are God's children.

Now if we are children, then we are heirs —heirs of God and co-heirs with Christ, if indeed we share in his sufferings in order that we may also share in his glory. I consider that our present sufferings are not worth comparing with the glory that will be revealed in us. The creation waits in eager expectation for the sons of God to be revealed.

Romans 8:15–19

WEEKEND

The Spirit helps us in our weakness. We do not
know what we ought to pray for, but the Spirit
himself intercedes for us with groans that words
cannot express. And he who searches our hearts
knows the mind of the Spirit, because the Spirit
intercedes for the saints in accordance with
God's will. And we know that in all things God
works for the good of those who love him, who
have been called according to his purpose.
For those God foreknew he also predestined to
be conformed to the likeness of his Son, that he
might be the firstborn among many brothers.
And those he predestined, he also called; those
he called, he also justified; those he justified, he
also glorified.

Romans 8:26–30

MONDAY

We know that if the earthly tent we live in is destroyed, we have a building from God, an eternal house in heaven, not built by human hands.

2 Corinthians 5:1

Stephen, full of the Holy Spirit, looked up to heaven and saw the glory of God, and Jesus standing at the right hand of God. "Look," he said, "I see heaven open and the Son of Man standing at the right hand of God."

Acts 7:55–56

Our citizenship is in heaven. And we eagerly await a Savior from there, the Lord Jesus Christ,

Philippians 3:20

TUESDAY

We believe that Jesus died and rose again and so
we believe that God will bring with Jesus those
who have fallen asleep in him. According to the
Lord's own word, we tell you that we who are
still alive, who are left till the coming of the
Lord, will certainly not precede those who have
fallen asleep. For the Lord himself will come
down from heaven, with a loud command, with
the voice of the archangel and with the trumpet
call of God, and the dead in Christ will rise first.
After that, we who are still alive and are left will
be caught up together with them in the clouds to
meet the Lord in the air. And so we will be with
the Lord forever. Therefore encourage each other
with these words.

1 Thessalonians 4:14–18

WEDNESDAY

Then I saw a new heaven and a new earth, for the
first heaven and the first earth had passed away,
and there was no longer any sea. I saw the Holy
City, the new Jerusalem, coming down out of
heaven from God, prepared as a bride beautifully
dressed for her husband. And I heard a loud voice
from the throne saying, "Now the dwelling of
God is with men, and he will live with them.
They will be his people, and God himself will be
with them and be their God. He will wipe every
tear from their eyes. There will be no more death
or mourning or crying or pain, for the old order
of things has passed away." He who was seated on
the throne said, "I am making everything new!"
Then he said, "Write this down, for these words
are trustworthy and true."

Revelation 21:1–5

THURSDAY

The Lord said to me: "It is done. I am the Alpha
and the Omega, the Beginning and the End. To
him who is thirsty I will give to drink without
cost from the spring of the water of life. He who
overcomes will inherit all this, and I will be his
God and he will be my son.

The angel carried me away in the Spirit to a
mountain great and high, and showed me the
Holy City, Jerusalem, coming down out of
heaven from God. It shone with the glory of
God, and its brilliance was like that of a very
precious jewel, like a jasper, clear as crystal. It
had a great, high wall with twelve gates, and with
twelve angels at the gates. On the gates were
written the names of the twelve tribes of Israel.

Revelation 21:6–7, 10–12

FRIDAY

I did not see a temple in the heavenly city, because the Lord God Almighty and the Lamb are its temple. The city does not need the sun or the moon to shine on it, for the glory of God gives it light, and the Lamb is its lamp. The nations will walk by its light, and the kings of the earth will bring their splendor into it. On no day will its gates ever be shut, for there will be no night there. The glory and honor of the nations will be brought into it. Nothing impure will ever enter it, nor will anyone who does what is shameful or deceitful, but only those whose names are written in the Lamb's book of life.

Revelation 21:22–27

WEEKEND

Then the angel showed me the river of the water
of life, as clear as crystal, flowing from the throne
of God and of the Lamb down the middle of the
great street of the city. On each side of the river
stood the tree of life, bearing twelve crops of
fruit, yielding its fruit every month. And the
leaves of the tree are for the healing of the
nations. No longer will there be any curse. The
throne of God and of the Lamb will be in the
city, and his servants will serve him. They will
see his face, and his name will be on their foreheads. There will be no more night. They will
not need the light of a lamp or the light of the
sun, for the Lord God will give them light. And
they will reign for ever and ever.

Revelation 22:1–5

MONDAY

Repent and be baptized, every one of you, in the name of Jesus Christ for the forgiveness of your sins. And you will receive the gift of the Holy Spirit. The promise is for you and your children and for all who are far off—for all whom the Lord our God will call.

Acts 2:38–39

You … were included in Christ when you heard the word of truth, the gospel of your salvation. Having believed, you were marked in him with a seal, the promised Holy Spirit, who is a deposit guaranteeing our inheritance until the redemption of those who are God's possession—to the praise of his glory.

Ephesians 1:13–14

This salvation, which was first announced by the Lord, was confirmed to us by those who heard him. God also testified to it by signs, wonders and various miracles, and gifts of the Holy Spirit distributed according to his will.

Hebrews 2:3–4

TUESDAY

There are different kinds of gifts, but the same
Spirit. There are different kinds of service, but
the same Lord. There are different kinds of
working, but the same God works all of them in
all men. Now to each one the manifestation of
the Spirit is given for the common good. To one
there is given through the Spirit the message of
wisdom, to another the message of knowledge by
means of the same Spirit, to another faith by the
same Spirit, to another gifts of healing by that
one Spirit, to another miraculous powers, to
another prophecy, to another distinguishing
between spirits, to another speaking in different
kinds of tongues, and to still another the inter-
pretation of tongues.

1 Corinthians 12:4–10

WEDNESDAY

All these [gifts] are the work of one and the same
Spirit, and he gives them to each one, just as he
determines. The body is a unit, though it is made
up of many parts; and though all its parts are
many, they form one body. So it is with Christ. ...
Now the body is not made up of one part but of
many. If the foot should say, "Because I am not a
hand, I do not belong to the body," it would not
for that reason cease to be part of the body. And
if the ear should say, "Because I am not an eye, I
do not belong to the body," it would not for that
reason cease to be part of the body.
If the whole body were an eye, where would the
sense of hearing be? If the whole body were an
ear, where would the sense of smell be? But in
fact God has arranged the parts in the body,
every one of them, just as he wanted them to be.
If they were all one part, where would the body
be? As it is, there are many parts, but one body.

1 Corinthians 12:11–12, 14–20

THURSDAY

To each one of us grace has been given as Christ apportioned it. This is why it says: "When he ascended on high, he led captives in his train and gave gifts to men." ... It was he who gave some to be apostles, some to be prophets, some to be evangelists, and some to be pastors and teachers, to prepare God's people for works of service, so that the body of Christ may be built up until we all reach unity in the faith and in the knowledge of the Son of God and become mature, attaining to the whole measure of the fullness of Christ.

Ephesians 4:7–8, 11–13

FRIDAY

We have different gifts, according to the grace
given us. If a man's gift is prophesying, let him
use it in proportion to his faith. If it is serving,
let him serve; if it is teaching, let him teach; if it
is encouraging, let him encourage; if it is con-
tributing to the needs of others, let him give generously; if it is leadership, let him govern
diligently; if it is showing mercy, let him do it
cheerfully.

Romans 12:6–8

WEEKEND

Jesus said, "I say to you: Ask and it will be given to you; seek and you will find; knock and the door will be opened to you. For everyone who asks receives; he who seeks finds; and to him who knocks, the door will be opened.
"Which of you fathers, if your son asks for a fish, will give him a snake instead? Or if he asks for an egg, will give him a scorpion? If you then, though you are evil, know how to give good gifts to your children, how much more will your Father in heaven give the Holy Spirit to those who ask him!"

Luke 11:9–13

MONDAY

The fruit of the Spirit is love, joy, peace, patience, kindness, goodness, faithfulness, gentleness and self-control. Against such things there is no law. Those who belong to Christ Jesus have crucified the sinful nature with its passions and desires. Since we live by the Spirit, let us keep in step with the Spirit.

Galatians 5:22–25

TUESDAY

Jesus said, "I am the true vine, and my Father is the gardener. He cuts off every branch in me that bears no fruit, while every branch that does bear fruit he prunes so that it will be even more fruitful. You are already clean because of the word I have spoken to you.

"Remain in me, and I will remain in you. No branch can bear fruit by itself; it must remain in the vine. Neither can you bear fruit unless you remain in me.

"I am the vine; you are the branches. If a man remains in me and I in him, he will bear much fruit; apart from me you can do nothing."

John 15:1–5

WEDNESDAY

Since the day we heard about you, we have not stopped praying for you and asking God to fill you with the knowledge of his will through all spiritual wisdom and understanding. And we pray this in order that you may live a life worthy of the Lord and may please him in every way: bearing fruit in every good work, growing in the knowledge of God, being strengthened with all power according to his glorious might so that you may have great endurance and patience, and joyfully giving thanks to the Father, who has qualified you to share in the inheritance of the saints in the kingdom of light.

Colossians 1:9–12

THURSDAY

Jesus said, "This is to my Father's glory, that you bear much fruit, showing yourselves to be my disciples.

"As the Father has loved me, so have I loved you. Now remain in my love. If you obey my commands, you will remain in my love, just as I have obeyed my Father's commands and remain in his love. I have told you this so that my joy may be in you and that your joy may be complete."

John 15:8–11

Through Jesus, … let us continually offer to God a sacrifice of praise—the fruit of lips that confess his name. And do not forget to do good and to share with others, for with such sacrifices God is pleased.

Hebrews 13:15–16

FRIDAY

This is my prayer: that your love may abound more and more in knowledge and depth of insight, so that you may be able to discern what is best and may be pure and blameless until the day of Christ, filled with the fruit of righteousness that comes through Jesus Christ—to the glory and praise of God.

Philippians 1:9–11

Live as children of light (for the fruit of the light consists in all goodness, righteousness and truth) and find out what pleases the Lord.

Ephesians 5:8–10

WEEKEND

Jesus said, "Every good tree bears good fruit, but a bad tree bears bad fruit. A good tree cannot bear bad fruit, and a bad tree cannot bear good fruit."

Matthew 7:17–18

Blessed is the man
    who does not walk in the counsel of the
      wicked
or stand in the way of sinners
    or sit in the seat of mockers.
But his delight is in the law of the LORD,
    and on his law he meditates day and night.
He is like a tree planted by streams of water,
    which yields its fruit in season
and whose leaf does not wither.
    Whatever he does prospers.

Psalm 1:1–3

MONDAY

I urge you, brothers, in view of God's mercy, to offer your bodies as living sacrifices, holy and pleasing to God—this is your spiritual act of worship. Do not conform any longer to the pattern of this world, but be transformed by the renewing of your mind. Then you will be able to test and approve what God's will is—his good, pleasing and perfect will.

Romans 12:1–2

TUESDAY

By the grace given me I say to every one of you:
Do not think of yourself more highly than you
ought, but rather think of yourself with sober
judgment, in accordance with the measure of
faith God has given you. Just as each of us has
one body with many members, and these members do not all have the same function, so in
Christ we who are many form one body, and
each member belongs to all the others.

Romans 12:3–5

WEDNESDAY

You ought to live holy and godly lives as you look forward to the day of God and speed its coming. That day will bring about the destruction of the heavens by fire, and the elements will melt in the heat. But in keeping with his promise we are looking forward to a new heaven and a new earth, the home of righteousness. So then, dear friends, since you are looking forward to this, make every effort to be found spotless, blameless and at peace with him.

2 Peter 3:11–14

THURSDAY

Love must be sincere. Hate what is evil; cling to what is good. Be devoted to one another in brotherly love. Honor one another above yourselves. Never be lacking in zeal, but keep your spiritual fervor, serving the Lord. Be joyful in hope, patient in affliction, faithful in prayer. Share with God's people who are in need. Practice hospitality.

Romans 12:9–13

FRIDAY

Bless those who persecute you; bless and do not
curse. Rejoice with those who rejoice; mourn
with those who mourn. Live in harmony with
one another. Do not be proud, but be willing to
associate with people of low position. Do not be
conceited. Do not repay anyone evil for evil. Be
careful to do what is right in the eyes of everybody. If it is possible, as far as it depends on you,
live at peace with everyone.

Romans 12:14–18

WEEKEND

Let no debt remain outstanding, except the con-
tinuing debt to love one another, for he who
loves his fellowman has fulfilled the law. The
commandments, "Do not commit adultery,"
"Do not murder," "Do not steal," "Do not
covet," and whatever other commandment there
may be, are summed up in this one rule: "Love
your neighbor as yourself." Love does no harm to
its neighbor. Therefore love is the fulfillment of
the law.

Romans 13:8–10

MONDAY

Peter was kept in prison, but the church was earnestly praying to God for him. The night before Herod was to bring him to trial, Peter was sleeping between two soldiers, bound with two chains, and sentries stood guard at the entrance. Suddenly an angel of the Lord appeared and a light shone in the cell. He struck Peter on the side and woke him up. "Quick, get up!" he said, and the chains fell off Peter's wrists. … They passed the first and second guards and came to the iron gate leading to the city. It opened for them by itself, and they went through it. When they had walked the length of one street, suddenly the angel left him.

Then Peter came to himself and said, "Now I know without a doubt that the Lord sent his angel and rescued me."

Acts 12:5–7, 10–11

TUESDAY

If you make the Most High your dwelling—
     even the LORD, who is my refuge—
then no harm will befall you,
     no disaster will come near your tent.
For he will command his angels concerning you
     to guard you in all your ways;
they will lift you up in their hands,
     so that you will not strike your foot against
          a stone.
You will tread upon the lion and the cobra;
     you will trample the great lion and the serpent.
"Because he loves me," says the LORD, "I will
          rescue him;
     I will protect him, for he acknowledges
          my name.
He will call upon me, and I will answer him;
     I will be with him in trouble,
     I will deliver him and honor him.
With long life will I satisfy him
     and show him my salvation."

Psalm 91:9–16

WEDNESDAY

When the servant of the man of God got up and
went out early the next morning, an army with
horses and chariots had surrounded the city.
"Oh, my lord, what shall we do?" the servant
asked.

"Don't be afraid," the prophet answered. "Those
who are with us are more than those who are
with them."

And Elisha prayed, "O LORD, open his eyes so he
may see." Then the LORD opened the servant's
eyes, and he looked and saw the hills full of
horses and chariots of fire all around Elisha.

2 Kings 6:15–17

THURSDAY

I, Daniel, mourned for three weeks. . . . and there before me was a man dressed in linen, with a belt of the finest gold around his waist. His body was like chrysolite, his face like lightning, his eyes like flaming torches, his arms and legs like the gleam of burnished bronze, and his voice like the sound of a multitude. . . .
A hand touched me and set me trembling on my hands and knees. He said, "Daniel, you who are highly esteemed, consider carefully the words I am about to speak to you, and stand up, for I have now been sent to you." And when he said this to me, I stood up trembling.
Then he continued, "Do not be afraid, Daniel. Since the first day that you set your mind to gain understanding and to humble yourself before your God, your words were heard, and I have come in response to them.

Daniel 10:2, 5–6, 10–12

FRIDAY

Jacob, ... had a dream in which he saw a stairway resting on the earth, with its top reaching to heaven, and the angels of God were ascending and descending on it.

There above it stood the LORD, and he said: "I am the LORD, the God of your father Abraham and the God of Isaac. I will give you and your descendants the land on which you are lying. Your descendants will be like the dust of the earth, and you will spread out to the west and to the east, to the north and to the south. All peoples on earth will be blessed through you and your offspring. I am with you and will watch over you wherever you go, and I will bring you back to this land. I will not leave you until I have done what I have promised you."

When Jacob awoke from his sleep, he thought, "Surely the LORD is in this place, and I was not aware of it." He was afraid and said, "How awesome is this place! This is none other than the house of God; this is the gate of heaven."

Genesis 28:12–17

WEEKEND

I saw the LORD seated on a throne, high and exalted, and the train of his robe filled the temple. Above him were seraphs, each with six wings: With two wings they covered their faces, with two they covered their feet, and with two they were flying.

And they were calling to one another: Holy, holy, holy is the LORD Almighty; the whole earth is full of his glory." At the sound of their voices the doorposts and thresholds shook and the temple was filled with smoke.

Isaiah 6:1–4

MONDAY

Praise be to the God and Father of our Lord Jesus Christ, who has blessed us in the heavenly realms with every spiritual blessing in Christ. For he chose us in him before the creation of the world to be holy and blameless in his sight. In love he predestined us to be adopted as his sons through Jesus Christ, in accordance with his pleasure and will—to the praise of his glorious grace, which he has freely given us in the One he loves.

Ephesians 1:3–6

TUESDAY

Christ redeemed us in order that the blessing
given to Abraham might come to the Gentiles
through Christ Jesus, so that by faith we might
receive the promise of the Spirit.

Galatians 3:14

All the peoples on earth will see that you are
called by the name of the LORD. . . . The LORD
will open the heavens, the storehouse of his
bounty, to send rain on your land in season and
to bless all the work of your hands.

Deuteronomy 28:10, 12

WEDNESDAY

"I will pour water on the thirsty land,
  and streams on the dry ground;" says the
    LORD,
"I will pour out my Spirit on your offspring,
  and my blessing on your descendants.
They will spring up like grass in a meadow,
  like poplar trees by flowing streams.

Isaiah 44:3–4

From the LORD comes deliverance.
  May your blessing be on your people, O LORD.

Psalm 3:8

You will be blessed in the city and blessed in the
country. The fruit of your womb will be blessed,
and the crops of your land. You will be blessed
when you come in and blessed when you go out.

Deuteronomy 28:3–4, 6

THURSDAY

From the fullness of God's grace we have all
received one blessing after another. For the law
was given through Moses; grace and truth came
through Jesus Christ.

John 1:16–17

"The fruit of righteousness will be peace;
    the effect of righteousness will be quietness
        and confidence forever,"
    says the LORD
"My people will live in peaceful dwelling places,
    in secure homes,
    in undisturbed places of rest. ...
how blessed you will be,
    sowing your seed by every stream."

Isaiah 32:17–18, 20

FRIDAY

When Jesus saw the crowds, he went up on a
mountainside and sat down. His disciples came
to him, and he began to teach them, saying:
"Blessed are the poor in spirit,
for theirs is the kingdom of heaven.
Blessed are those who mourn,
for they will be comforted.
Blessed are the meek,
for they will inherit the earth.
Blessed are those who hunger and thirst for
righteousness,
for they will be filled.
Blessed are the merciful,
for they will be shown mercy.
Blessed are the pure in heart,
for they will see God.
Blessed are the peacemakers,
for they will be called sons of God.
Blessed are those who are persecuted because
of righteousness,
for theirs is the kingdom of heaven."

Matthew 5:1–10

WEEKEND

The LORD bless you
    and keep you;
the LORD make his face shine upon you
    and be gracious to you;
the LORD turn his face toward you
    and give you peace.

Numbers 6:24–26

"I will send down showers in season; there will be showers of blessing," says the LORD. "The trees of the field will yield their fruit and the ground will yield its crops; the people will be secure in their land."

Ezekiel 34:26–27

MONDAY

Whatever was to my profit I now consider loss
for the sake of Christ. What is more, I consider
everything a loss compared to the surpassing
greatness of knowing Christ Jesus my Lord, for
whose sake I have lost all things. I consider them
rubbish, that I may gain Christ and be found in
him, not having a righteousness of my own that
comes from the law, but that which is through
faith in Christ—the righteousness that comes
from God and is by faith.

Philippians 3:7–9

TUESDAY

I want to know Christ and the power of his resurrection and the fellowship of sharing in his
sufferings, becoming like him in his death, and
so, somehow, to attain to the resurrection from
the dead. Not that I have already obtained all
this, or have already been made perfect, but I
press on to take hold of that for which Christ
Jesus took hold of me.

Philippians 3:10–12

WEDNESDAY

I do not consider myself yet to have taken hold
of it. But one thing I do: Forgetting what is
behind and straining toward what is ahead, I
press on toward the goal to win the prize for
which God has called me heavenward in Christ
Jesus. All of us who are mature should take such
a view of things. And if on some point you think
differently, that too God will make clear to you.

Philippians 3:13–15

THURSDAY

Our citizenship is in heaven. And we eagerly
await a Savior from there, the Lord Jesus Christ
who, by the power that enables him to bring
everything under his control, will transform our
lowly bodies so that they will be like his glorious
body. Therefore, my brothers, you whom I love
and long for, my joy and crown, that is how you
should stand firm in the Lord, dear friends!

Philippians 3:20—4:1

FRIDAY

I know what it is to be in need, and I know what
it is to have plenty. I have learned the secret of
being content in any and every situation,
whether well fed or hungry, whether living in
plenty or in want. I can do everything through
Christ who gives me strength.

Philippians 4:12–13

Therefore, since through God's mercy we have
this ministry, we do not lose heart.

2 Corinthians 4:1

WEEKEND

Let us acknowledge the LORD;
    let us press on to acknowledge him.
As surely as the sun rises,
    he will appear;
he will come to us like the winter rains,
    like the spring rains that water the earth.

Hosea 6:3

Let us not become weary in doing good, for at
the proper time we will reap a harvest if we do
not give up.

Galatians 6:9

MONDAY

If God is for us, who can be against us? He who
did not spare his own Son, but gave him up for
us all —how will he not also, along with him,
graciously give us all things? Who will bring any
charge against those whom God has chosen? It is
God who justifies.

Romans 8:31–33

TUESDAY

Christ Jesus, who died—more than that, who was
raised to life—is at the right hand of God and is
also interceding for us. Who shall separate us from
the love of Christ? Shall trouble or hardship or
persecution or famine or nakedness or danger or
sword? As it is written: For your sake we face
death all day long; we are considered as sheep to
be slaughtered."
No, in all these things we are more than con-
querors through him who loved us.

Romans 8:34–37

WEDNESDAY

For I am convinced that neither death nor life,
neither angels nor demons, neither the present
nor the future, nor any powers, neither height
nor depth, nor anything else in all creation, will
be able to separate us from the love of God that
is in Christ Jesus our Lord.

Romans 8:38–39

Christ redeemed us from the curse of the law by
becoming a curse for us.

Galatians 3:13

THURSDAY

"For I know the plans I have for you," declares
the LORD, "plans to prosper you and not to harm
you, plans to give you hope and a future. Then
you will call upon me and come and pray to me,
and I will listen to you. You will seek me and
find me when you seek me with all your heart. I
will be found by you," declares the LORD.

Jeremiah 29:11–14

God made Christ who had no sin for us, so that in
him we might become the righteousness of God.

2 Corinthians 5:21

FRIDAY

Those who trust in the LORD are like
    Mount Zion,
    which cannot be shaken but endures forever.
As the mountains surround Jerusalem,
    so the LORD surrounds his people
    both now and forevermore.

Psalm 125:1–2

This is how we know what love is: Jesus Christ
laid down his life for us.

1 John 3:16

For God did not appoint us to suffer wrath but
to receive salvation through our Lord Jesus
Christ. He died for us so that, whether we are
awake or asleep, we may live together with him.

1 Thessalonians 5:9–10

WEEKEND

The LORD your God is the one who goes with
you to fight for you against your enemies to give
you victory.

Deuteronomy 20:4

Who is this King of glory?
    The LORD strong and mighty,
    the LORD mighty in battle.
Lift up your heads, O you gates;
    lift them up, you ancient doors,
    that the King of glory may come in.
Who is he, this King of glory?
    The LORD Almighty—
    he is the King of glory.
To you, O LORD, I lift up my soul;
    in you I trust, O my God.
Do not let me be put to shame,
    nor let my enemies triumph over me.
No one whose hope is in you
    will ever be put to shame. . . .

Psalm 24:8—25:3

MONDAY

For God, who said, "Let light shine out of darkness," made his light shine in our hearts to give us the light of the knowledge of the glory of God in the face of Christ."
But we have this treasure in jars of clay to show that this all-surpassing power is from God and not from us.
We are hard pressed on every side, but not crushed; perplexed, but not in despair; persecuted, but not abandoned; struck down, but not destroyed. We always carry around in our body the death of Jesus, so that the life of Jesus may also be revealed in our body. For we who are alive are always being given over to death for Jesus' sake, so that his life may be revealed in our mortal body.

2 Corinthians 4:6–11

TUESDAY

We do not lose heart. Though outwardly we are wasting away, yet inwardly we are being renewed day by day. For our light and momentary troubles are achieving for us an eternal glory that far out-weighs them all. So we fix our eyes not on what is seen, but on what is unseen. For what is seen is temporary, but what is unseen is eternal. Now we know that if the earthly tent we live in is destroyed, we have a building from God, an eter-nal house in heaven, not built by human hands.

2 Corinthians 4:16—5:1

WEDNESDAY

Meanwhile we groan, longing to be clothed with our heavenly dwelling, because when we are clothed, we will not be found naked. For while we are in this tent, we groan and are burdened, because we do not wish to be unclothed but to be clothed with our heavenly dwelling, so that what is mortal may be swallowed up by life. Now it is God who has made us for this very purpose and has given us the Spirit as a deposit, guaranteeing what is to come.

2 Corinthians 5:2–5

THURSDAY

O LORD, you are our Father.
  We are the clay, you are the potter;
  we are all the work of your hand.

Isaiah 64:8

We are God's workmanship, created in Christ
Jesus to do good works, which God prepared in
advance for us to do.

Ephesians 2:10

May you be blessed by the LORD,
  the Maker of heaven and earth.

Psalm 115:15

FRIDAY

I saw the LORD seated on a throne, high and
exalted, and the train of his robe filled the temple. Above him were seraphs, each with six
wings: With two wings they covered their faces,
with two they covered their feet, and with two
they were flying. And they were calling to one
another: "Holy, holy, holy is the LORD Almighty;
the whole earth is full of his glory."
At the sound of their voices the doorposts and
thresholds shook and the temple was filled with
smoke.
"Woe to me!" I cried. "I am ruined! For I am a
man of unclean lips, . . . and my eyes have seen
the King, the LORD Almighty."
Then one of the seraphs flew to me with a live
coal in his hand, which he had taken with tongs
from the altar. With it he touched my mouth
and said, "See, this has touched your lips; your
guilt is taken away and your sin atoned for."
Then I heard the voice of the LORD saying,
"Whom shall I send? And who will go for us?"
And I said, "Here am I. Send me!"

Isaiah 6:1–8

WEEKEND

As a father has compassion on his children,
   so the LORD has compassion on those who fear him;
for he knows how we are formed,
   he remembers that we are dust.

Psalm 103:13–14

If there is a natural body, there is also a spiritual body. So it is written: "The first man Adam became a living being" ; the last Adam, a life-giving spirit. The spiritual did not come first, but the natural, and after that the spiritual. The first man was of the dust of the earth, the second man from heaven. As was the earthly man, so are those who are of the earth; and as is the man from heaven, so also are those who are of heaven. And just as we have borne the likeness of the earthly man, so shall we bear the likeness of the man from heaven.

1 Corinthians 15:44–49

MONDAY

Carry each other's burdens, and in this way you will fulfill the law of Christ. If anyone thinks he is something when he is nothing, he deceives himself. Each one should test his own actions. Then he can take pride in himself, without comparing himself to somebody else, for each one should carry his own load.

Galatians 6:2–5

TUESDAY

Let us not become weary in doing good, for at
the proper time we will reap a harvest if we do
not give up. Therefore, as we have opportunity,
let us do good to all people, especially to those
who belong to the family of believers.

Galatians 6:9–10

The one who sows to please the Spirit, from the
Spirit will reap eternal life.

Galatians 6:8

WEDNESDAY

None of us lives to himself alone . . . we belong to the Lord.

Romans 14:7–8

Live in harmony with one another; be sympathetic, love as brothers, be compassionate and humble.

1 Peter 3:8

The wisdom that comes from heaven is first of all pure; then peace-loving, considerate, submissive, full of mercy and good fruit, impartial and sincere. Peacemakers who sow in peace raise a harvest of righteousness.

James 3:17–18

THURSDAY

The kingdom of God is not a matter of eating and drinking, but of righteousness, peace and joy in the Holy Spirit, because anyone who serves Christ in this way is pleasing to God and approved by men. Let us therefore make every effort to do what leads to peace and to mutual edification.

Romans 14:17–19

We ought always to thank God for you, brothers, and rightly so, because your faith is growing more and more, and the love every one of you has for each other is increasing.

2 Thessalonians 1:3

Each of us will give an account of himself to God. ... Make up your mind not to put any stumbling block or obstacle in your brother's way.

Romans 14:12–13

FRIDAY

The entire law is summed up in a single command: "Love your neighbor as yourself."

Galatians 5:14

"If you are offering your gift at the altar and there remember that your brother has something against you, leave your gift there in front of the altar. First go and be reconciled to your brother; then come and offer your gift.

Matthew 5:23–24

WEEKEND

Jesus said to the disciples, "You are the salt of the earth."

Matthew 5:13

Jesus said, "Salt is good, but if it loses its saltiness, how can you make it salty again? Have salt in yourselves, and be at peace with each other."

Mark 9:50

Now that you have purified yourselves by obeying the truth so that you have sincere love for your brothers, love one another deeply, from the heart. For you have been born again, not of perishable seed, but of imperishable, through the living and enduring word of God.

1 Peter 1:22–23

MONDAY

Jesus said, "Just as the living Father sent me and I live because of the Father, so the one who feeds on me will live because of me. This is the bread that came down from heaven. . . . He who feeds on this bread will live forever."

John 6:57–59

On the first day of the Feast of Unleavened Bread, the disciples came to Jesus . . . While they were eating, Jesus took bread, gave thanks and broke it, and gave it to his disciples, saying, "Take and eat; this is my body."

Matthew 26:17, 26

TUESDAY

The people asked Jesus, "What must we do to do the works God requires?"

Jesus answered, "The work of God is this: to believe in the one he has sent."

So they asked him, "What miraculous sign then will you give that we may see it and believe you? What will you do? Our forefathers ate the manna in the desert; as it is written: 'He gave them bread from heaven to eat.'"

Jesus said to them, "I tell you the truth, it is not Moses who has given you the bread from heaven, but it is my Father who gives you the true bread from heaven. For the bread of God is he who comes down from heaven and gives life to the world."

"Sir," they said, "from now on give us this bread."

Then Jesus declared, "I am the bread of life. He who comes to me will never go hungry, and he who believes in me will never be thirsty."

John 6:28–35

WEDNESDAY

Remember how the LORD your God led you all
the way in the desert these forty years, to humble
you and to test you in order to know what was in
your heart, whether or not you would keep his
commands. He humbled you, causing you to
hunger and then feeding you with manna, which
neither you nor your fathers had known, to teach
you that man does not live on bread alone but
on every word that comes from the mouth of the
LORD.

Deuteronomy 8:2–5

THURSDAY

"Come, all you who are thirsty,
   come to the waters;
and you who have no money,
   come, buy and eat!
Come, buy wine and milk
   without money and without cost," says the
      LORD.
"Why spend money on what is not bread,
   and your labor on what does not satisfy?
Listen, listen to me, and eat what is good,
   and your soul will delight in the richest of fare.
Give ear and come to me;
   hear me, that your soul may live."

Isaiah 55:1–3

FRIDAY

"As the rain and the snow
  come down from heaven,
and do not return to it
  without watering the earth
and making it bud and flourish,
    so that it yields seed for the sower and bread
      for the eater,
so is my word that goes out from my mouth:
    It will not return to me empty," declares the
      LORD,
"but will accomplish what I desire
  and achieve the purpose for which I sent it.
You will go out in joy
  and be led forth in peace;
the mountains and hills
  will burst into song before you,
and all the trees of the field
  will clap their hands."

Isaiah 55:10–12

WEEKEND

Jesus said, "No one can come to me unless the Father who sent me draws him, . . . I tell you the truth, he who believes has everlasting life. I am the bread of life. Your forefathers ate the manna in the desert, yet they died. But here is the bread that comes down from heaven, which a man may eat and not die. I am the living bread that came down from heaven. If anyone eats of this bread, he will live forever."

John 6:44, 47–51

MONDAY

Jesus said, "Do you not say, 'Four months more
and then the harvest'? I tell you, open your eyes
and look at the fields! They are ripe for harvest.
Even now the reaper draws his wages, even now
he harvests the crop for eternal life, so that the
sower and the reaper may be glad together.
Thus the saying 'One sows and another reaps' is
true. I sent you to reap what you have not
worked for. Others have done the hard work,
and you have reaped the benefits of their labor."

John 4:35–38

TUESDAY

Jesus told [the people] many things in parables, saying: "A farmer went out to sow his seed. As he was scattering the seed, some fell along the path, and the birds came and ate it up. Some fell on rocky places, where it did not have much soil. It sprang up quickly, because the soil was shallow. But when the sun came up, the plants were scorched, and they withered because they had no root. Other seed fell among thorns, which grew up and choked the plants. Still other seed fell on good soil, where it produced a crop—a hundred, sixty or thirty times what was sown."

Matthew 13:3–8

WEDNESDAY

Jesus said, "Listen then to what the parable of the sower means: When anyone hears the message about the kingdom and does not understand it, the evil one comes and snatches away what was sown in his heart. This is the seed sown along the path. The one who received the seed that fell on rocky places is the man who hears the word and at once receives it with joy. But since he has no root, he lasts only a short time. When trouble or persecution comes because of the word, he quickly falls away. The one who received the seed that fell among the thorns is the man who hears the word, but the worries of this life and the deceitfulness of wealth choke it, making it unfruitful. But the one who received the seed that fell on good soil is the man who hears the word and understands it. He produces a crop, yielding a hundred, sixty or thirty times what was sown."

Matthew 13:18–23

THURSDAY

Peacemakers who sow in peace raise a harvest of righteousness.

James 3:18

No discipline seems pleasant at the time, but painful. Later on, however, it produces a harvest of righteousness and peace for those who have been trained by it.

Hebrews 12:11

Now he who supplies seed to the sower and bread for food will also supply and increase your store of seed and will enlarge the harvest of your righteousness. You will be made rich in every way so that you can be generous on every occasion, and through us your generosity will result in thanksgiving to God.

2 Corinthians 9:10–11

FRIDAY

Jesus told [the disciples], "The harvest is plentiful, but the workers are few. Ask the Lord of the harvest, therefore, to send out workers into his harvest field."

Luke 10:2

Let us not become weary in doing good, for at the proper time we will reap a harvest if we do not give up. Therefore, as we have opportunity, let us do good to all people, especially to those who belong to the family of believers.

Galatians 6:9–10

WEEKEND

Be glad, O people of Zion,
    rejoice in the LORD your God,
for he has given you
    the autumn rains in righteousness.
He sends you abundant showers,
    both autumn and spring rains, as before.
The threshing floors will be filled with grain;
    the vats will overflow with new wine and oil.
"I will repay you for the years the locusts
        have eaten—
    the great locust and the young locust,
    the other locusts and the locust swarm—
my great army that I sent among you.
You will have plenty to eat, until you are full,
    and you will praise the name of the LORD
        your God,
    who has worked wonders for you;
never again will my people be shamed.

Joel 2:23–26

MONDAY

We know that in all things God works for the good of those who love him, who have been called according to his purpose. For those God foreknew he also predestined to be conformed to the likeness of his Son, that he might be the first-born among many brothers. And those he predestined, he also called; those he called, he also justified; those he justified, he also glorified.

Romans 8:28-30

TUESDAY

In Christ we have redemption through his blood, the forgiveness of sins, in accordance with the riches of God's grace that he lavished on us with all wisdom and understanding. And he made known to us the mystery of his will according to his good pleasure, which he purposed in Christ, to be put into effect when the times will have reached their fulfillment—to bring all things in heaven and on earth together under one head, even Christ. In him we were also chosen, having been predestined according to the plan of him who works out everything in conformity with the purpose of his will, in order that we, who were the first to hope in Christ, might be for the praise of his glory.

Ephesians 1:7–12

WEDNESDAY

The LORD will fulfill his purpose for me;
>your love, O LORD, endures forever—
>do not abandon the works of your hands.

Psalm 138:8

Many are the plans in a man's heart,
>but it is the LORD's purpose that prevails.

Proverbs 19:21

Ah, Sovereign LORD, you have made the heavens
and the earth by your great power and out-
stretched arm. Nothing is too hard for you. You
show love to thousands but bring the punishment for the fathers' sins into the laps of their
children after them. O great and powerful God,
whose name is the LORD Almighty, great are
your purposes and mighty are your deeds.

Jeremiah 32:17–19

THURSDAY

Jesus said, "This, then, is how you should pray:
"'Our Father in heaven, hallowed be your name,
your kingdom come, your will be done on earth
as it is in heaven.'"

Matthew 6:9–10

You ought to say, "If it is the Lord's will, we will
live and do this or that."

James 4:15

Jesus prayed, "My Father, if it is not possible for
this cup to be taken away unless I drink it, may
your will be done."

Matthew 26:42

FRIDAY

This is what the LORD says:
"Stand at the crossroads and look;
    ask for the ancient paths,
ask where the good way is, and walk in it,
    and you will find rest for your souls.
    But you said, 'We will not walk in it.'"

Jeremiah 6:16

"Call to me and I will answer you and tell you
great and unsearchable things you do not know,"
says the LORD.

Jeremiah 33:3

Trust in the LORD with all your heart
    and lean not on your own understanding;
in all your ways acknowledge him,
    and he will make your paths straight.

Proverbs 3:5–6

WEEKEND

For from Christ and through Christ and to
Christ are all things. To him be the glory forever!
Amen. Therefore, I urge you, brothers, in view
of God's mercy, to offer your bodies as living sacrifices, holy and pleasing to God—this is your
spiritual act of worship. Do not conform any
longer to the pattern of this world, but be transformed by the renewing of your mind. Then you
will be able to test and approve what God's will
is—his good, pleasing and perfect will.

Romans 11:36—12:2

MONDAY

Arise, shine, for your light has come,
    and the glory of the LORD rises upon you.
See, darkness covers the earth
    and thick darkness is over the peoples,
but the LORD rises upon you
    and his glory appears over you.
Nations will come to your light,
    and kings to the brightness of your dawn.
"Lift up your eyes and look about you:
    All assemble and come to you;
your sons come from afar,
    and your daughters are carried on the arm.
Then you will look and be radiant,
    your heart will throb and swell with joy;
the wealth on the seas will be brought to you,
    to you the riches of the nations will come.

Isaiah 60:1–5

TUESDAY

You are my lamp, O LORD;
    the LORD turns my darkness into light.

2 Samuel 22:29

The precepts of the LORD are right,
    giving joy to the heart.
The commands of the LORD are radiant,
    giving light to the eyes.

Psalm 19:8

The LORD is my light and my salvation—
    whom shall I fear?

Psalm 27:1

WEDNESDAY

O LORD, you preserve both man and beast.
　　How priceless is your unfailing love!
Both high and low among men
　　find refuge in the shadow of your wings.
They feast on the abundance of your house;
　　you give them drink from your river of
　　　　delights.
For with you is the fountain of life;
　　in your light we see light.
Continue your love to those who know you,
　　your righteousness to the upright in heart.

Psalm 36:6–10

THURSDAY

In the beginning was the Word, and the Word was with God, and the Word was God. He was with God in the beginning. Through him all things were made; without him nothing was made that has been made. In him was life, and that life was the light of men. The light shines in the darkness, but the darkness has not understood it.

There came a man who was sent from God; his name was John. He came as a witness to testify concerning that light, so that through him all men might believe. He himself was not the light; he came only as a witness to the light. The true light that gives light to every man was coming into the world.

John 1:1–9

FRIDAY

Everything exposed by the light becomes visible, for it is light that makes everything visible. This is why it is said:
"Wake up, O sleeper,
    rise from the dead,
and Christ will shine on you."

Ephesians 5:13–14

Jesus said, "You are the light of the world. A city on a hill cannot be hidden. Neither do people light a lamp and put it under a bowl. Instead they put it on its stand, and it gives light to everyone in the house. In the same way, let your light shine before men, that they may see your good deeds and praise your Father in heaven."

Matthew 5:14–16

WEEKEND

The [heavenly] city does not need the sun or the
moon to shine on it, for the glory of God gives it
light, and the Lamb is its lamp. The nations will
walk by its light, and the kings of the earth will
bring their splendor into it. On no day will its
gates ever be shut, for there will be no night there.

Revelation 21:23–25

The sun will no more be your light by day,
    nor will the brightness of the moon shine on you,
for the LORD will be your everlasting light,
    and your God will be your glory.
Your sun will never set again,
    and your moon will wane no more;
the LORD will be your everlasting light,
    and your days of sorrow will end.

Isaiah 60:19–20

MONDAY

Jesus said, "What shall we say the kingdom of God is like, or what parable shall we use to describe it? It is like a mustard seed, which is the smallest seed you plant in the ground. Yet when planted, it grows and becomes the largest of all garden plants, with such big branches that the birds of the air can perch in its shade."

Mark 4:30–32

Jesus said, "If you have faith as small as a mustard seed, you can say to this mulberry tree, 'Be uprooted and planted in the sea,' and it will obey you."

Luke 17:6

TUESDAY

Jesus said, "The kingdom of heaven is like a net that was let down into the lake and caught all kinds of fish. When it was full, the fishermen pulled it up on the shore. Then they sat down and collected the good fish in baskets, but threw the bad away. This is how it will be at the end of the age. The angels will come and separate the wicked from the righteous."

Matthew 13:47–49."

WEDNESDAY

Jesus also said, "This is what the kingdom of God is like. A man scatters seed on the ground. Night and day, whether he sleeps or gets up, the seed sprouts and grows, though he does not know how. All by itself the soil produces grain— first the stalk, then the head, then the full kernel in the head. As soon as the grain is ripe, he puts the sickle to it, because the harvest has come."

Mark 4:26–29

THURSDAY

Jesus said, "The kingdom of heaven is like treasure hidden in a field. When a man found it, he hid it again, and then in his joy went and sold all he had and bought that field.

"Again, the kingdom of heaven is like a merchant looking for fine pearls. When he found one of great value, he went away and sold everything he had and bought it."

Matthew 13:44–47

Jesus said, "Whoever wants to save his life will lose it, but whoever loses his life for me and for the gospel will save it."

Mark 8:35

FRIDAY

Jesus told them another parable: "The kingdom of heaven is like a man who sowed good seed in his field. But while everyone was sleeping, his enemy came and sowed weeds among the wheat, and went away. When the wheat sprouted and formed heads, then the weeds also appeared.

"The owner's servants came to him and said, 'Sir, didn't you sow good seed in your field? Where then did the weeds come from?'

"'An enemy did this,' he replied.

"The servants asked him, 'Do you want us to go and pull them up?'

"'No,' he answered, 'because while you are pulling the weeds, you may root up the wheat with them. Let both grow together until the harvest. At that time I will tell the harvesters: First collect the weeds and tie them in bundles to be burned; then gather the wheat and bring it into my barn.'"

Matthew 13:24–30

WEEKEND

Jesus said, "Suppose a woman has ten silver coins
and loses one. Does she not light a lamp, sweep
the house and search carefully until she finds it?
And when she finds it, she calls her friends and
neighbors together and says, 'Rejoice with me; I
have found my lost coin.' In the same way, I tell
you, there is rejoicing in the presence of the
angels of God over one sinner who repents."

Luke 15:8–10

MONDAY

The LORD is my rock, my fortress and my
    deliverer;
    my God is my rock, in whom I take refuge.
He is my shield and the horn of my salvation,
    my stronghold.

Psalm 18:2

The LORD alone is my rock and my salvation;
    he is my fortress, I will not be shaken.
My salvation and my honor depend on God;
    he is my mighty rock, my refuge.

Psalm 62:6–7

TUESDAY

Come, let us sing for joy to the LORD;
> let us shout aloud to the Rock of our salvation.

Let us come before him with thanksgiving
> and extol him with music and song.

For the LORD is the great God,
> the great King above all gods.

Psalm 95:1–3

Trust in the LORD forever,
> for the LORD, the LORD, is the Rock eternal.

Isaiah 26:4

WEDNESDAY

"This is what the LORD says—
>   Israel's King and Redeemer, the LORD
>   Almighty:
I am the first and I am the last;
>   apart from me there is no God.
Who then is like me? Let him proclaim it.
>   Let him declare and lay out before me
what has happened since I established my
>   ancient people,
>   and what is yet to come—
>   yes, let him foretell what will come.
Do not tremble, do not be afraid.
>   Did I not proclaim this and foretell it
>   long ago?
You are my witnesses. Is there any God
>   besides me?
>   No, there is no other Rock; I know not one."

Isaiah 44:6–8

THURSDAY

We are God's fellow workers; you are God's field, God's building. By the grace God has given me, I laid a foundation as an expert builder, and someone else is building on it. But each one should be careful how he builds. For no one can lay any foundation other than the one already laid, which is Jesus Christ.

1 Corinthians 3:9–11

From the ends of the earth I call to you, LORD,
  I call as my heart grows faint;
    lead me to the rock that is higher than I.

Psalm 61:2

FRIDAY

Jesus said, "Everyone who hears these words of mine and puts them into practice is like a wise man who built his house on the rock. The rain came down, the streams rose, and the winds blew and beat against that house; yet it did not fall, because it had its foundation on the rock. "But everyone who hears these words of mine and does not put them into practice is like a foolish man who built his house on sand. The rain came down, the streams rose, and the winds blew and beat against that house, and it fell with a great crash."

Matthew 7:24–27

WEEKEND

As you come to him, the living Stone—rejected
by men but chosen by God and precious to
him—you also, like living stones, are being built
into a spiritual house to be a holy priesthood,
offering spiritual sacrifices acceptable to God
through Jesus Christ. For in Scripture it says:
"See, I lay a stone in Zion,
    a chosen and precious cornerstone,
and the one who trusts in him
    will never be put to shame."

1 Peter 2:4–6

MONDAY

The LORD will take delight in you,
    and your land will be married.
As a young man marries a maiden,
    so will your sons marry you;
as a bridegroom rejoices over his bride,
    so will your God rejoice over you.

Isaiah 62:4–5

I delight greatly in the LORD;
    my soul rejoices in my God.
For he has clothed me with garments of salvation
    and arrayed me in a robe of righteousness,
as a bridegroom adorns his head like a priest,
    and as a bride adorns herself with her jewels.

Isaiah 61:10

TUESDAY

"Your Maker is your husband—
    the LORD Almighty is his name—
the Holy One of Israel is your Redeemer;
    he is called the God of all the earth.
The LORD will call you back
    as if you were a wife deserted and distressed
        in spirit—
a wife who married young,
    only to be rejected," says your God.
"For a brief moment I abandoned you,
    but with deep compassion I will bring
        you back.
In a surge of anger
    I hid my face from you for a moment,
but with everlasting kindness
    I will have compassion on you,"
    says the LORD your Redeemer.

Isaiah 54:5–8

WEDNESDAY

I saw the Holy City, the new Jerusalem, coming
down out of heaven from God, prepared as a
bride beautifully dressed for her husband. And I
heard a loud voice from the throne saying, "Now
the dwelling of God is with men, and he will live
with them. They will be his people, and God
himself will be with them and be their God. He
will wipe every tear from their eyes. There will be
no more death or mourning or crying or pain,
for the old order of things has passed away." He
who was seated on the throne said, "I am making
everything new!" Then he said, "Write this
down, for these words are trustworthy and true."

Revelation 21:2–5

THURSDAY

One of the seven angels ... came and said to me,
"Come, I will show you the bride, the wife of the
Lamb." And he carried me away in the Spirit to a
mountain great and high, and showed me the
Holy City, Jerusalem, coming down out of
heaven from God. It shone with the glory of
God, and its brilliance was like that of a very
precious jewel, like a jasper, clear as crystal. It
had a great, high wall with twelve gates, and with
twelve angels at the gates. On the gates were
written the names of the twelve tribes of Israel.
There were three gates on the east, three on the
north, three on the south and three on the west.
The wall of the city had twelve foundations, and
on them were the names of the twelve apostles of
the Lamb.

Revelation 21:9–14

FRIDAY

Husbands ought to love their wives as their own bodies. He who loves his wife loves himself. After all, no one ever hated his own body, but he feeds and cares for it, just as Christ does the church— for we are members of his body. "For this reason a man will leave his father and mother and be united to his wife, and the two will become one flesh." This is a profound mystery—but I am talking about Christ and the church.

Ephesians 5:28–32

WEEKEND

Then I heard what sounded like a great multitude, like the roar of rushing waters and like loud peals of thunder, shouting:
"Hallelujah!
    For our Lord God Almighty reigns.
Let us rejoice and be glad
    and give him glory!
For the wedding of the Lamb has come,
    and his bride has made herself ready.
Fine linen, bright and clean,
    was given her to wear."
(Fine linen stands for the righteous acts of the
    saints.)
Then the angel said to me, "Write: 'Blessed are those who are invited to the wedding supper of the Lamb!' And he added, "These are the true words of God."

Revelation 19:6–9

MY FAVORITE VERSES...

_____

_____

_____

_____

_____

_____

_____

_____

_____

_____

_____

_____

_____

_____

_____

_____

_____

_____

_____